FAITH AND REASON

FAITH AND REASON

by
NATHANIEL MICKLEM
M.A., LL.D., D.D.
Sometime Principal of Mansfield College, Oxford

ἔστιν θάλασσα, τίς δέ νιν κατασβέσει;

GERALD DUCKWORTH & CO. LTD.
3 Henrietta Street, London, W.C.2

First published 1963
© NATHANIEL MICKLEM 1963

PRINTED IN GREAT BRITAIN
BY EBENEZER BAYLIS AND SON, LTD.
THE TRINITY PRESS, WORCESTER, AND LONDON

CONTENTS

6 *Contents*

INTRODUCTION

THERE must be a radical reconstruction of Christian thought if the Christian religion is to offer any acceptable answer to the intellectual issues of the present day and is to play that part in the future history of the world to which all Christians must suppose it to be called.

This radical reconstruction is required of us for four reasons in particular. First, the notable advances in mathematics, in physics, in psychology and in the study of non-Christian religions have greatly enlarged and made enormously more mysterious the scope of the world we have to contemplate. Second, the agony through which the world has been passing during these years, as represented by Hiroshima and Belsen, by genocide and the millions of refugees, by a return to barbarism among peoples long regarded as civilized and by the turmoil of Asia and Africa, has shattered the secure world of thought complacently accepted fifty years ago. Third, the Christian faith must be directly related to the 'atheism' proclaimed by the Communism which, in spite of the political tyranny with which it has been associated in practice, has appealed to the idealism of many in this generation. Fourth, the theologian must meet the deepest challenge which comes from within the field of faith when the most genial of theologians, Professor Karl Barth (the iron is in his theology, not in his temper and address), proclaims the revelation of God as the abolition of religion, and Dietrich Bonhoeffer, theologian and martyr, could write from prison of a 'religionless Christianity'.

The theologian today cannot always turn to the philo-

sophers for help. In the great poem of his old age, to which
I shall make frequent reference, Robert Bridges complained
that

> Philosophy
> filtering out delusions from her theory of life,
> in dread of superstition gave religion away
> to priests and monks, who rich in their monopoly
> furbish and trim the old idols, that they dare not break,
> for fear of the folk and need of good disciplin[1].

The charge has substance, but philosophy itself has in this
last generation largely renounced its high vocation as the
pursuit of wisdom and fulfilled to the letter the prophetic
observation of Seneca long ago, *quae philosophia fuit, facta
philologia est*;[2] that which was once the pursuit of wisdom
has become the cult of the English lexikon.

In such a new world of wonder, of terror and of bewilder-
ment it is not surprising that scepticism like an arctic
winter has descended upon the minds of many in the West.
An old Greek elegiac couplet states it well:

> πάντα γέλως καὶ πάντα κόνις καὶ πάντα τὸ μηδέν,
> πάντα γάρ ἐξ ἀλόγων ἐστι τὰ γινόμενα

or, as it may be paraphrased in English, life is an unhappy
joke, human beings are no more significant than a cloud of
dust, and the universe is not merely irrational, it is a
nothingness. In a new and chaotic situation of this kind it is
idle for Christians to repeat the old dogmatic shibboleths
adhaerendo maioribus, *credendo credentibus*, as if the old
world had not passed away.

The following pages are not to be regarded as an essay in
apologetics. No man can be argued into becoming a mathematician or a chemist or a musician or a religious person.
Anyone with sufficient intelligence can acquire information

---

[1] *The Testament of Beauty*, IV. 1139 ff.   [2] *Ep.* 108. 23.

on these subjects; he can learn the language, but he will never understand until he has gradually felt his way into a world of thought that has been unfamiliar to him. I have attempted to set out the Christian faith in language generally intelligible and in a form not incompatible with modern knowledge. I am not offering some new religious fancies of my own as a substitute for the historic faith of Christendom, for the Christian faith is what it is, not what I or any other may be pleased to think it ought to be. Neither am I attempting to trick out traditional, orthodox doctrines in a new dress more appropriate to the fashion of the day. It is written in the Bible that 'Jesus Christ is the same yesterday, today and for ever', and that he is 'the Way, the Truth and the Life'. I shall make plain in the sequel how I understand these words, but they express in lapidary form the faith to which I am committed.

This frank, initial admission of my presupposition or commitment may help to conciliate the anxious Christian reader but may cause the rationalist or sceptical reader to proceed no further; for what, he will ask, can I say to him whose presuppositions are so very different? We cannot usefully argue about that which we presuppose, but I accept Dr. Bartley's demand that we expose our beliefs and conjectures and traditions and presuppositions to the most searching criticism, that we may counteract and eliminate as much intellectual error as is possible.[1] If the rationalist and sceptical reader will adopt this attitude also, I will hope that he may venture further into this book. 'Not a few of our latter-day intellectuals,' wrote John Baillie, '. . . may indeed be found protesting that they have rid themselves of the last vestigial shred of faith, the life they live being unaffected by any clue to its ultimate meaning. But I am by no means always inclined to take their word for this, for it is open to me, without discourtesy, to suspect that they are incorrectly

[1] *The Retreat to Commitment*, esp. Ch. V.

analysing their own spiritual condition. I should look to their deeds as well as to their words, to their behaviour when they are off their intellectual guard as well as to their merely theoretical conclusions about themselves.'[1] Saint-Beuve could compare his intelligence to 'a dead moon that bathes in its cold rays the cemetery of his heart', and many today might seem in like case with him; yet a man wholly without capacity for religion would, I think, lack one of the distinctive characteristics of humanity, and I rarely look into a human face without thinking that I detect beneath its lines and its expression a touch of the infinite in the form of longing or of heartbreak or, it may be, of thankfulness. I have made no attempt to demonstrate the faith of Christians but have sought to indicate that if we will follow the logic of our hearts or, rather, of our whole personalities and not merely the syllogisms of the textbooks, we shall see, because we are human, that Jesus the Christ is *expectatio gentium et desideratus earum*,[2] he for whom the peoples look and he who meets their deepest need.

But where shall I begin? Dr. Karl Barth, the great dogmatic theologian of our time, would start unhesitatingly from the Bible. 'The basic theological question,' writes Dr. Paul Tillich on the other hand, 'is the question of God. God is the answer to the question implied in being';[3] I should start, therefore, from 'being', a term that covers everything that is, for to the logician, as Professor J. B. Hawkins says, being signifies most obviously 'instantiation'.[4] Dr. Nels Ferré, again, in his notable book, *The Christian Understanding of God*, starts from the Christian apprehension of God as Love and, in distinction from those who in the past have attempted to express the Christian faith in the thought-forms of Plato, of Aristotle, of Hegel or some other philo-

---

[1] *The Sense of the Presence of God*, p. 77.
[2] A conflation, I admit, from two of the Advent introits.
[3] *Systematic Theology*, I. 181.
[4] *Prospect for Metaphysics*, ed. I. Ramsey, p. 114.

sopher, has sought to formulate a distinctively Christian philosophy upon the basis of this single premiss.

I have not been able to follow any of these routes. I cannot begin with the Bible, for I must first enquire what is the nature of its authority, and why I should accept it. I cannot start from 'being', for I do not come to religion through metaphysics, nor, as I shall shew, can I start from Nature, for man is a baffling mystery to himself, and physicists and biologists in spite of all their learning have made the rest of Nature far more mysterious than ever it was before; moreover, as Kemp Smith said, 'by no idealization of the creaturely can we transcend the creaturely',[1] or, as John Oman put it, 'there is no possibility of starting from sensation and arriving at a poet's perception'.[2] Finally, I cannot start with Dr. Ferré, for, though I agree with him that the apprehension of God as Love is the ultimate intuition of the illuminated mind as it is grasped by what Professor Tillich in the language of Plotinus calls an ecstasy of reason, I must first try to make plain what we mean by this word 'God'.

I have been moved (as who has not?) by the rolling, majestic argument of St. Thomas Aquinas wherein he proves that God is, that he is one, simple, eternal, loving. To these assurances, supposedly accessible to man's natural reason, there have customarily been added certain 'truths of revelation' or at least 'articles of faith' made known from heaven by a supernatural illumination granted to the apostles and others of high spiritual privilege. This traditional basis of theology has been undermined. We may, perhaps, be able to shew that the Absolute or the Unconditioned or the Transcendent is a necessary postulate of thought, but the existence and attributes of 'God', if the word be taken in any religious sense, cannot be proved by irrefutable logic. Further, theologians no longer claim that certain 'truths' in

[1] Quoted J. Baillie, *op. cit.*, p. 117.
[2] *The Natural and the Supernatural*, p. 168.

the form of theological propositions are mysteriously vouch-safed from heaven. There is no answering le Roy: 'if dogmas formulated absolute truth in adequate terms, they would be unintelligible to us. If they only gave an imperfect truth relative and changing, their imposition could not be legitimate'.[1]

This admission, however, does not involve that the Christian profession is irrational. We must distinguish between *ratio discursiva* and *ratio intuitiva*; the discursive reason is that which starting from certain admitted pre-misses moves from point to point and concludes with a logical or, as it is sometimes called, a scientific demonstration. The intuitive reason, on the other hand, is the faculty whereby we apprehend first principles such as, for instance, the law of contradiction or the obligation of duty or in the realm of poetry the relative merits of Shakespeare and of Mrs. Hemans, for here we have rational certainties which can be seen but never can be proved.

I often think that Christians, except perhaps those rare, enchanted spirits, if such there be, who inhabit beatitude as their permanent dwelling, are like the flying fish which leap out of the water into the sun but in a moment failing to maintain their poise sink back into the sea. Most Christians glimpse the glory of God only in rare moments and at inter-vals, 'and glory both in the later Old Testament and in the New is really only another word for presence'.[2] It is a mis-fortune that the Christian religion is usually discussed as if it were a *corpus* of doctrine, whereas in fact it might be better described as a series of intimations or of insights.

> Just when we're safest, there's a sunset-touch,
> A fancy from a flower-bell, some one's death,
> A chorus-ending from Euripides,
> And that's enough for fifty hopes and fears—
> The grand Perhaps.[3]

[1] *Dogme et Critique*, p. 23.   [2] J. Baillie, *op. cit.*, p. 260.
[3] R. Browning, *Bishop Blougram's Apology*.

I find that, as I grow older, I see everything with an increasing astonishment and wonder. There is, of course, the ever-recurrent miracle of nature, of the hedges and of the fields and of the woods; then there is the strange mystery of human life with its threads and entanglements and splendours; there hovers over it all the shadow of death which none may escape and which seems in one aspect so final and in another, as I think, a home-going. Again, there is the oppressive, unintelligible weight of human suffering, and there is the mystery of Beauty and of Goodness and of Forgiveness. As I have written elsewhere:

> In each perceived existence, in that aught
> Exists (what is Existence?), in that Space
> And vagrant Time conspiring should have brought
> From out the Void this moment and this place,
> These scents of hedgerow and this violet's grace,
> Yon ploughshare left on some forgetful night—
> Who shall the pattern and the secret trace
> Of such aeonian riddle, every mite
> Whereof is charged and lustred by the Infinite?[1]

I have written in the following pages of that which, as I am very certain, I have seen; yet I would echo the words of the psalmist (in our traditional version), 'such knowledge is too wonderful for me; it is high; I cannot attain unto it'. I suffer from that manner or temperament or nature which Charles Williams has called 'the quality of disbelief'. This quality, he tells us, comes directly from the Creed and (not that this has anything to do with me) is quite compatible with sanctity; 'yet undoubtedly it also involves as much disbelief as possible; it allows for, it encourages, the sense of agnosticism and the possibility of error'.[2] 'I conceive,' wrote Henry More, the Cambridge Platonist, 'that we may give full assent to that which notwithstanding may possibly be otherwise'.[3] It was the one dictator known in our history

---

[1] From *The Labyrinth*. [2] *The Descent of the Dove*, pp. 189 f.
[3] *The Antidote against Atheism*, ed. II. 1665, p. 4.

who said, 'I beseech you by the bowels of Christ to believe
it possible you may be mistaken.' But I fall back again on
Browning:

> I am a wanderer; I remember well
> One journey, how I feared the track was missed,
> So long the city I desired to reach
> Lay hid, when suddenly its spires afar
> Flashed through the circling clouds; you may conceive
> My transport; soon the vapours closed again,
> But I had seen the city, and one such glance
> No darkness could obscure.[1]

I am quite sure we have seen 'the glory of God in the face
of Jesus Christ'; I am equally sure we cannot prove it.

As regards this book I have not been able to detect anything original in its pages, except, of course, that each man
must find his own way as best he can. I have styled my
chapters 'lectures' for such they are in form and manner;
they are lectures undelivered, not so much through any lack
of opportunity as chiefly because of the disabilities of Public
Transport. To my great advantage, and still more to the
advantage of the reader, I am no longer surrounded by
bookshelves nor am I within easy reach of learned libraries.
I have been prevented, therefore, from bespattering my
pages with footnotes offering a spurious parade of erudition.
Many relevant books I have never read, and of those I have
read I have forgotten more than I remember; but a man's
education has been defined as that which he knows when he
has forgotten all that he was taught at school, and if the
pleasant habit of giving Greek titles to English books had
not long since been abandoned, I should be disposed to call
this little volume HUPOMNEMATA GERONTOS, which would
mean the latter reflections of one who has lived longer than
the psalmist thought convenient.

I have, however, quoted freely. I set out from two

[1] *Paracelsus* Pt. IV.

volumes published by Duckworth more than fifty years ago, Dean Rashdall's *Philosophy and Religion*, a statement of 'Personal Idealism', and Dean Inge's *Faith and its Psychology*, an exposition, as the writer claims, of a 'moderate realism'; for these two, different as they are, may be taken to represent free, radical and pioneering Christian thought before the catastrophe of the First World War. The two most massive and independent thinkers in the intervening years, to my limited knowledge, have been my revered mentor, John Oman, of Westminster College, Cambridge, and Professor Paul Tillich who is still teaching in America— *serus redeat in coelum*. I shall also be found to have plundered extensively, but I hope with forgiveness, from Professor Polanyi and with the connivance of the Clarendon Press from the poet, Robert Bridges. Other quotations are often introduced chiefly by way of respite, for in a long speech there should be pauses,

> *neque semper arcum*
> *tendit Apollo.*

I have to thank my friend, Dr. A. W. Whitehouse of the University of Durham for commenting upon one chapter for me and to my venerable friend, our most learned living theologian, Dr. R. S. Franks, for commenting upon and amending several chapters.

I have done what I could but am not satisfied. In Mervyn Peake's macabre novel *Gormenghast* Dr. Prunesquallor's sister says to him, ' "I get so tired of the way you say things. And I don't really like the things you say." "Irma," (said her brother) "nor do I. They always sound stale by the time I hear them. The brain and the tongue are so far apart." '[1] Moreover, all the things that most we want to say 'break through language and escape', and it does not occur to me that in these days of intellectual confusion I

[1] p. 82.

have always written wisely, nor that my argument at best can be more than a very temporary notice-board indicating structural alterations in the roadway.

N.M.

Monks Staithe,
  Princes Risborough.
    February 1963.

Part I

RELIGION

I—NATURE

RASHDALL ON MATTER AND CAUSE

In his lectures entitled *Philosophy and Religion* Rashdall proffers 'aids to educated men desirous of thinking out for themselves a reasonable basis for personal religion'.[1] He does not claim to produce an unchallengeable proof of the Christian religion, but 'for purposes of life it is entirely reasonable to treat probabilities as certainties'.[2] He holds that all religious truth depends logically upon inference,[3] and that the existence, the goodness, the providence of God together with the expectation of life after death can be logically inferred from nature and from life as we experience them. His arguments are set forth with clarity and force; they are intimately related to the *philosophia perennis* which in its Christian form comes to us through St. Augustine and St. Thomas, and they represent the apologetic defence of theism which still largely commends itself to Christian apologists. Not without affectionate thoughts of my old tutor and friend, I must indicate where it is to be found inadequate today.

Starting from the distinction between mind and matter he asks whether matter can be taken for a substance which could be considered as existing altogether apart from any kind of conscious experience.[4] In matter he recognizes two elements; there are the qualities that we know by sensation, and there are certain relations such as the spatial and temporal. All the sensible qualities of things depend upon senses for their apprehension, but it is mind which recog-

[1] p. ix.   [2] p. 132.   [3] p. 138.   [4] p. 8.

nizes colour, scent, sound, solidity and the like. Similarly
all the relations of matter require mind for their apprehension. Newcastle, we say, is north of London, but the
northness, so to call it, is not located in Newcastle nor in
any intervening point; it is a relation between two places
apprehended by a mind. Matter, therefore, is essentially
related to mind, but since no human mind nor all human
minds together are aware of all the matter that is and has
been in the universe, we must infer the existence of a
supreme Mind, which we call God. 'There is no nature
except by reason of Thy knowing it,' said St. Augustine.[1]

In his second lecture Rashdall treats of 'the Universal
Cause'. For every event, he says,[2] there must be a cause.
Whence do we derive this idea of 'cause'? If I by an act of
will pick up a stone, hurl it at a window and, my aim being
satisfactory, smash the window, I may claim to have caused
the débris that results. We derive our idea of cause, says
Rashdall, from acts of our volition; cause is correlative to
will. Causality, he continues, is a postulate of science.
Natural science depends upon experiment, and experi-
menting presupposes this idea of cause. If, therefore, cause
is correlative to will, not only must we posit cause in the
world of nature, but the uniformity of nature compels us to
posit an universal cause, and therefore an universal will;
this universal Cause like the universal Mind we may call
God.

We may agree that we cannot sensibly speak about a
universe without some conscious or unconscious reference
to a spectator. There can be no 'here' or 'there' except in
respect of an observer, nor, I suppose, can there be a
'before' and 'after' unless there be some one to mark the
lapse of time. If we prescind from the universe all those
aspects of colour, scent, sound and solidity which are
correlative to human senses, and eliminate 'here' and 'there',

[1] *Conf.* VII. 4.   [2] p. 37.

'before' and 'after' together with any mind to apprehend a pattern or series of patterns in the whirling of those electrons which are surmised by science, the universe as we know it has disappeared. That there is a universe which existed before man was and extends indefinitely beyond our present comprehension is undeniable. And since that which is not merely unknown but is intrinsically unknowable cannot be said in any intelligible sense to exist, or to have existed, or, in other words, since by existence we mean existence for Mind, it seems we must postulate Mind or something corresponding to a Knower for which the universe exists. A religious word like 'God', however, carries connotations which the argument has not justified. Such a Knower may be a necessary postulate of thought, but the nature of such a Being is wholly incomprehensible to us; a philosophical postulate is not God.

But the age-old controversy between Mind and Matter, with which Rashdall deals, has now grown out of date. Not merely has the concept of mind grown vastly more complicated in the light of the researches and speculations of medical psychologists, but the very idea of matter has evaporated under the scrutiny of the physicists. Matter, it would appear, is a form of energy; '*matter* is where the concentration of energy is great,' wrote Einstein, '*field* where the concentration of energy is small.'[1] The philosopher F. C. S. Schiller, a generation ago could poke fun at the *otium cum dignitate* of 'the thing in itself',[2] but 'the thing in itself' has now become energy, and it passes the wit of man to understand how there can be energy if nothing is being energetic. We now find it convenient to speak of 'particles' as ultimate units where in earlier days men spoke of atoms, but a particle is a most elusive entity; if it is divisible it is not an ultimate unit, and if it is not divisible it is not

[1] *The Evolution of Physics*, p. 256.
[2] *The Riddle of the Sphinx*, p. 32.

material at all; we are further told that it may have position
or it may have velocity, but both it cannot have. The
physicist will tell us, I think, that a particle is not an entity
that can be envisaged; it is, rather, something that must be
postulated and conceived in such a way that terms like
divisibility and indivisibility cannot apply to it; in fact, it is
not in the traditional sense material at all. Or what, we may
ask, is an electron? It is not a particle, says Professor
Coulson, though it may often be convenient to treat it as if
it were; nor on the other hand is it a wave, which is a form
of motion, though on other occasions it may most conveniently be so regarded.[1] We must not even say that it is
an electric somewhat, for it is not strictly a material object.
So fugitive and evasive has 'matter' become that the
origin of all things is now sometimes ascribed to that which
is called 'Space-Time'. Physics ends in mysticism or at
least in impenetrable mystery.

In respect of 'cause' also I should judge that Rashdall has
taken too great a leap. It may be true that we first become
aware of the idea of causation through our own volitional
initiative as we may first become aware of time through the
consciousness of memory, but our sense that of necessity
everything must have a cause cannot be derived from our
realization that certain ends we can achieve by our acts of
will. Nor would it ever occur to us (apart from theological
preconception) that all causes are acts of will. Causation, I
feel sure, is, like time and space, a category in terms of
which by the structure of the human mind we experience
the world. If we ask, as any child may ask, what causes the
rainbow in the sky, the answer will be the light of the sun
passing through raindrops and refracted in the human eye.
Have we here one cause or three causes, the sunlight, the
raindrops and the eye? It would be absurd to say that the
rainbow has no cause, but we can say no more than that

[1] *Science and Christian Belief*, pp. 37 f.

when the sunlight passes through raindrops and the light so refracted is received by the retina of the eye, a human being sees a rainbow; no question of 'will' arises or occurs to any one.

Nor is it true that everything has a cause, if by a cause we mean a single cause. If taking deliberate aim I have thrown a stone at a window and smashed the glass, the primary cause of the breakage may be said to be an act of will, but certainly the friability of glass, the density of the stone and the excellence of my aim will be contributory causes. Again, the same event may be the result of wholly divergent 'causes'. The mental picture of a yellow colour, for instance, is 'caused' in me by seeing a golden object, by hearing the word 'gold' spoken, by seeing the word in print or feeling it in Braille. While we cannot get away from the category of causation, scientists, I think, avoid the word 'cause' so far as possible, even though causation is presupposed in every experiment they make. They will tell us that given certain factors a, and b, and c, and d, a certain result e, will almost certainly occur. I say 'almost certainly' because even in laboratories very odd things occur or fail to occur, and science has come to use such phrases as 'random mutation' and 'chance variation'; moreover, it is claimed by Heisenberg that the invalidity of the causal law is definitely proved by quantum mechanics; 'According to the Heisenberg "principle of Indeterminacy" the behaviour of the particles of which the physical world consists, is not causally controlled. Science has reached the unexpected and perplexing conclusion that identical conditions do not necessarily lead to identical results, that the same state of things may give rise to different consequences, and since various events may follow, what will actually take place cannot be foretold.'[1] Even so, we cannot escape from the idea of cause, for when the same conditions fail to produce the same result, this

[1] W. Macneile Dixon, *The Human Situation*, p. 352, Penguin ed.

failure, we say, is *caused* by the unpredictable behaviour of electrons. The 'laws of nature' in fact are generalizations; they are not of themselves an immutable element in the structure of the universe.

We must say, however, that the whole universe, because it is a rational order to be explored by reason, cannot be a chance affair and in that sense must have a cause. We might agree, then, with Rashdall that we must postulate some First Cause, but the term 'cause' is so obscure that to ascribe the origin of the universe to a First Cause is no more intelligible than to ascribe it to Space-Time, for in both cases we are ascribing the origin of *things* to the categories of *thought* in terms of which we experience the world. 'Belief in causality as a necessary principle,' writes Professor H. D. Lewis, 'is tantamount to a belief in God.'[1] This is Rashdall's point, but 'God' is a religious term and unsuitable in this place. There must, indeed, be a Ground of existence, and this term, 'Ground', is far preferable here because, as Tillich says, it 'oscillates between cause and substance and transcends both'.[2]

THE FUNCTION OF SCIENCE

It is easy but superficial to point out that energy without something energetic, that vibration without something that vibrates, that a particle which is both indivisible and at the same time material, that saddle-shaped space, that electricity without something charged therewith is nonsense. So it is, but the scientists are not talking nonsense. They are performing their proper task, and the advances of physics in the last generation or so must rank among the great achievements of the human mind. The function of science is popularly misunderstood. The notion that what the scientists say is true has taken the place of the older ideas that

[1] *Prospect for Metaphysics*, p. 230.   [2] *Systematic Theology*. I. 173

what the Bible or what the Pope says is true. The scientists, as I understand them, make no such claim. They look, they measure, they experiment, and then in the light of all the available data and by the exercise of a trained and sometimes inspired imagination they propound that theory which in their judgement will best account for the facts which lie before them. The task of science is σώζειν τὰ φαινόμενα or 'saving the appearances'. The scientists are dealing with phenomena, that is, with appearances. Their presuppositions are manifold and indemonstrable; they assume that the world is intelligible; they assume that 'the laws of nature' do not change; they operate with concepts such as motion, time, space and causation, which are not physical. Newtonian physics offered a far more rational and satisfactory account of phenomena than had been achieved before; the phenomena are better saved, or the appearances are better accounted for, in terms of relativity or the quantum theory. No doubt yet wider generalizations and more satisfactory theories will be proffered in due time. The scientists are probing an actual world that underlies, and is hidden from, our senses, but of what it is ultimately composed, of what is that 'matter', if it can be called matter, which is the substance of all physical phenomena, of what is that reality beneath all the appearances which they study they cannot tell; they profess a wise agnosticism. We should be very foolish to claim that it is given to theologians to mend their learned ignorance. 'Matter' and 'cause' remain impenetrable mystery.

The argument from 'matter' and from 'cause' has led us no farther than this, that we must postulate a Ground of the universe and some manner of Knower for which or for whom all that is knowable exists. But we can go further. The universe as we know it cannot be the result of Chance; it bears throughout the clear marks of an Intelligence such as is reflected in the mind of man.

THE UNIVERSE NOT DUE TO CHANCE

The universe cannot be the work of Chance. On the railway station at Abergele (I borrow my illustration from Professor Polanyi)[1] the name of the place is tricked out in large letters composed of little pebbles. No sane person will suppose that these pebbles fell into precisely this configuration by mere accident. It would be an absurdity on a cosmic scale to suppose that the intricate and complicated patterns, the astonishing mutual adaptations, the vast generalizations covered by algebraic formulae called 'the laws of nature' are due to blind and unoccasioned chance. The old mechanical determinism of Newtonian physics has been abandoned by the scientists; the contingent, the unpredictable is constantly occurring, and scientific prediction can never ascend above the highest degree of probability; but the universe as revealed by science is quite plainly an order, an immense complication of patterns, a Whole informed by inscrutable Intelligence.

Inscrutable indeed, but inscrutable Intelligence. A. E. Taylor says somewhere that the discoveries of modern science have vastly fortified the old 'argument from Design', one of the traditional arguments for God's existence, and to this we may agree provided it be granted that it is only here and there and in the most limited degree that we can trace the great Design, and that 'God' be not taken here in a religious sense.

Science can describe but can offer no sort of explanation. A few simple instances may be permitted. My first is from Rachel Carson's *The Sea Around Us*:[2] the grunion is a small fish which in some inexplicable and wholly mysterious fashion is aware of the monthly cycle whereby certain tides are higher than at other times. Shortly after the full moon from March to August the grunion come in to the shore

[1] *Personal Knowledge*, pp. 33 f. [2] pp. 163 f. Penguin ed.

just when the high tides begin to ebb; they allow themselves to be carried up on to the wet sand of the beach on the crest of one wave, and casting themselves into the wash of the next they are swept out to sea again. In the brief pause between the two waves the act of spawning is performed. The eggs are left buried in the sand; the tide now receding leaves them there. Within a fortnight the larval fish are fully formed within the egg; at the next high tide the sand is washed away, the membranes rupture, and the little fish are carried out to sea. That this might happen once by chance could be imagined, that it happens year after year, generation after generation, cannot be by accident. Behind such a repeated, constant achievement we observe the operation of that which in some obscure sense we must call Intelligence or Mind.

My second illustration shall be the gorgeous peacock. The peacock's tail is decorated with a series of perfect 'eyes'; these 'eyes' are constructed out of hundreds of feathers with thousands of separate branches. How and why does the peacock achieve this feat? I think the 'why' is as mysterious as the 'how'. We read of 'protective colouring' and sexual attraction, but why and how precisely this pattern, and this pattern every time? Where is the intelligence that plans and provides such splendour?

> Who taught the nations of the field and wood
> To shun their poison, and to choose their food?
> Prescient, the tides or tempest to withstand,
> Build on the wave, or arch beneath the sand?
> Who made the spider parallels design
> Sure as de Moivre, without rule or line?
> Who bade the stork, Columbus-like, explore
> Heavens not his own, and worlds unknown before?
> Who calls the council, states the certain day,
> Who forms the phalanx, and who points the way?

Professor Dixon, who in his Gifford Lectures recounted with uncommon eloquence, range and felicity the marvels revealed by modern science, quotes the scientist Jennings: 'if Amoeba were the size of a dog, instead of being micro-scopic, no one would deny to its actions the name of intelligence'.[1] Or

> Consider the tiny egg-shell whence man groweth,
> how it proliferateth freely, as a queen-bee doth,
> and more surely than any animal or plant breedeth;
> how each offspring cell is for some special work
> differentiated and functioneth spontaneously,
> and ev'n wil change its predetermin'd faculty
> when accidental environment maketh a call,
> leaving its proper sphere to amend what hath gone wrong:
> Consider then their task, those unimaginable
> infinit co-adaptations of function'd tissue
> correlated delicately in a ravel'd web
> of unknown sensibilities . . . how 'tis a task
> incomparable in complexity with whatsoe'er
> the bees can boast; nor do the unshapely cells behave
> with lesser show of will, nor of purpose and skill:
> Pass by the rarer achievements, yes, forget all fames,
> all works all art all virtue and knowledge—set them by,
> and still the solved problems must exhaust our wonder.[2]

So the physician-poet describes the marvels of the human embryo, but this is no unique wonder, for, as he later says:[3]

> All terrestrial life, in all functions and motions,
> operateth thru alliance of living entities
> disparate in their structure but logically
> correlated in action under some final cause.
> Suchlike co-ordinations may be acquired in man
> with reason'd purpose consciently, as when a learner
> on viol or flute diligently traineth his hand
> to the intricat fingering of the stops and strings;
> or may be innate, as the spontaneous flight of birds;
> or antenatal and altogether inconscient,
> as the food-organs, called vegetativ because
> such cellular connivance is the life of plants.

[1] *The Human Situation*, p. 137. Penguin ed.
[2] Robert Bridges. *The Testament of Beauty*. II. 266 ff.
[3] *ib*. IV. 781 ff.

CREATIVITY AND PURPOSE

For all that science can tell to the contrary there may be something corresponding in some dim way to thought or memory in plants and even atoms. As physicists and biologists trace for us the story of evolution from original units, whatever we suppose them to be, to ever more differentiated elements and wholes and then the development of life from the virus-like speck to the protozoon, to multicellular organisms, to the arrival of a nervous system, of sense-organs followed by noogenesis and then anthropogenesis, evolution appears plainly as a feat of emergence.[1] 'Existence,' writes Dr. Raven, 'is less like a struggle than an adventure.'[2] 'Creativity is expressed in the properties and functioning of the elements themselves, atom molecule, mass; cell, structure, organism.'[3] Professor Polanyi's phrase, 'the originative powers of unconscious thought'[4] echoes Robert Bridges' 'the speechless intuitions of inconscient mind'.[5]

Robert Bridges seems justified, then, in speaking of 'some final cause', for the creative *nisus* is to be apprehended in the whole as in each part; the evolution which we can trace upon this planet is a concurrent and interlocked performance; moreover the process seems irreversible, for, as Oman grimly points out, life may have begun in the water, but if a man tries to return to life in the water, he becomes a corpse and not a fish.[6] It is, so to put it, apparently a pull from before, not a push from behind, that is indicated in the process. Teilhard de Chardin's account of evolution as a groping, a guided groping, as he calls it, was anticipated by the poet,

---

[1] *v.* Polanyi, *op. cit.*, p. 390.
[2] *Experience and Interpretation*, p. 135.   [3] *ib.*, p. 143.
[4] *op. cit.*, p. 339.   [5] *Testament of Beauty*, II. 711.
[6] *The Natural and the Supernatural*, p. 294.

> If Selfhood thus rule thru'out organic life
> 'tis no far thought that all the dumb activities
> in atom and molecule are like phenomena
> of individual Selfhood in its first degrees.

If there is both Intelligence and Motion or Process, and if that Process is informed by Intelligence, it would seem that purpose is involved, and that the universe, which is an unity and a whole, subtends some purpose, which may be called the Cause of causes or the Final Cause. The scientist describes, the philosopher may speculate, but the traditional easy answer of the theologians is impossible today. It has been traditionally taught that God made all things for man, and man for himself. This is pre-Copernican theology, though it still finds its adherents. If by man we mean man as we know him upon this planet, is it conceivable that the Milky Way and the unnumbered galaxies which science has calculated or surmised were made for man? Is it for man's sake that, as they tell me, a molecule of hydrogen must perform four hundred and fifty rotations every second? Upon what ground should we suppose that horses and dogs and wasps and woodlice have no significance apart from their significance for man? This is one of the points where a revolutionary change is required of theological reflection. The universe can no longer be regarded as the stage, the setting, the changing scenery for the drama of human life and of redemption. The universe with the story of evolution represents a vast and unimaginable drama wherein we on this planet for a few short years must play our part without rehearsal and without any knowledge of the plot's beginning or its end. We know now that man is but a speck upon a planet which of itself is but a drop in the ocean of the universe. It is these very necessary considerations which most of all have made the dogmatisms of traditional Christianity incredible.

THE EMERGENCE OF MAN

But the most remarkable thing we know about matter or Nature or whatever we like to call it is that at last it has thrown up man. Can mind, asks Professor Dixon, be an accident in nature, could reason arise from an irrational universe, how can a brain know that it is a brain?[1] Nature produced man, yet till man arose there was no 'Nature'. I do not mean that till man arrived there was nothing there, but what was there? Geologists always describe that remote past in terms of what man would have seen had man been there to see, but before there was a percipient, nothing was seen, nor can we intelligibly speak of light and dark, or of hot and cold, of large and small, of long or short. We may speak, if we will, of swirling masses of electrons, but what electrons are we do not know; we may say, if we will, that our world existed for the 'Mind' for which all things exist; but *omne recipitur secundum modum recipientis*; we know how the world looks to us who apprehend it through our senses, but of what the world 'looks like' to Universal Mind we can form no conception. So far as we can tell, it is man only in the universe who has the concept of Nature, and in whose mind, imperfectly but ever more perfectly, Nature is reflected as in a mirror. Nature, as it were, becomes aware of herself in man; the mystery of Reason is parallel to the mystery of Nature, for apart from the rational self there is no consciousness or thinking, no desiring and no explaining, no science, no logic, no knowing and no being known.[2]

We may take the wonder one step further. We judge Nature to be transient, contingent and imperfect. This can only be because Nature has given rise in us to the notion of the eternal, the necessary and the perfect. We could not speak of imperfection had we no conception of the perfect nor of the changing had we no sense of the changeless.

[1] *op. cit.*, pp. 71 ff.   [2] *v.* Dixon, *op. cit.*, p. 346.

Logically, but not chronologically, our ideals, our sense of
the Transcendent, are given *a priori*. More, it is for man,
says Oman, to stand on the ground of what is and to reach
out from it to what ought to be; this 'is only possible for a
person, and is in the measure in which he is independent;
but this presupposes an universe which responds to such
independence and is only really known by it, which means
that it also is in some true sense personal'.[1]

The universe, then, we must reckon to be an order; it is
rational in that it is to be apprehended and studied by man's
reason and it corresponds thereto; so far as we can closely
study it, it must be seen as conative, a process of emergence
through response to environment; it is an expression of
Intelligence and must be deemed in some obscure sense
personal.

> *Spiritus intus alit, totamque infusa per artus*
> *Mens agitat molem et magno se corpore miscet,*[2]

or, as the Christian poet puts it,

> From Universal Mind the first-born atoms draw
> their function, whose rich chemistry the plants transmute
> to make organic life whereon animals feed
> to fashion sight and sense and give service to man,
> who sprung from them is conscient in his last degree
> of ministry unto God, the Universal Mind,
> whither all effect returneth whence it first began.[3]

THE IDEA OF 'GOD'

But can we properly speak of Universal Mind as God?
Hitherto except in quotation I have kept to such terms as
'the Transcendent', 'the Absolute', 'the Ground of Existence', 'the Universal Mind'. All these phrases point to that
which thought is bound to postulate but that which cannot

---

[1] *The Natural and the Supernatural*, pp. 339 f.
[2] *Aeneid*. VI. 726 f.
[3] *The Testament of Beauty*, IV. 116–122.

be envisaged or imagined. The religious term is 'God', by which we mean the Transcendent contemplated as an object of worship. To be religious, writes Professor H. D. Lewis, is 'to apprehend a "beyond" which thought cannot reach but which thought itself requires for its completion.'[1] We may accept this definition if by 'apprehension' we understand some emotional as well as intellectual response to this 'beyond'; for worship, which means the ascription of worthship, is more than a merely intellectual attitude; and to considerations of worth we have not come yet; therefore we may not yet properly speak of 'God'.

But if this 'beyond' is apprehended as Universal Mind, it must be conceived, so far as it can be conceived at all, in personal terms rather than impersonal, as Him rather than as It; yet, except when we are using the symbolical language of poetry or piety, we must not speak of the Transcendent as a Person, for this would represent him as one person, no doubt supreme and far more than human, but still one person amongst others. The Transcendent or God is not a being alongside others; he is the Ground of all existence. ' "Personal God",' writes Tillich, 'does not mean that God is *a* person. It means that God is the ground of everything personal, and that he carries within himself the onto-logical power of personality.'[2]

There are those who like to speak of God as a Super-person, and there is no objection to that if it be thought meaningful. Perhaps 'the divine Spirit' best serves our purpose. That 'Spirit' is an indefinable term is not, in this context, a disadvantage; moreover it is suggested by Virgil in the passage quoted above, it is Biblical, for 'God is Spirit',[3] and the term is familiar to philosophers through Hegel; it has this further advantage over such terms as 'Absolute', 'Infinite' and 'Unconditioned' that it is, so to say, an active

---

[1] *Prospect for Metaphysics*, p. 226.   [2] *Systematic Theology*, II. 291.
[3] *John*, IV. 24.

noun. Professor H. H. Farmer criticizes Oman for speaking so often of the Super-natural 'in a way that suggests that it is a merely static environment which man becomes aware of, explores and gets to know through his sense of sacred values'.[1] Spirit is 'the unity of power and meaning.'[2]

The Super-natural or Transcendent in fact, is known to us through some sort of encounter; 'being personal,' writes Farmer, 'the encounter involves activity on both sides, on the one hand a divine initiative of self-disclosure towards man and, on the other hand, man's self-conscious apprehension of, and response to, that approach.'[3] So C. C. J. Webb speaks of a 'consciousness of a personal relation between ourselves and the Higher than ourselves in whose presence we stand'.[4] 'I would see in the religious experience of mankind as a whole a genuine unity,' he writes elsewhere, 'and would consider it as the response of the human spirit to a Divine Spirit with which it is by the necessity of its nature in perpetual contact.'[5]

An awareness of God, says Tillich, is present in the question of God; in other words, we could not raise the question of the Transcendent unless we were aware of it; of the infinite we are aware only through the finite, and in this awareness man who is finite transcends his finitude.[6] We must be aware of the touch of the divine Spirit before we can usefully discuss theology; we must be

> as a man set down
> In some strange jeopardy of enormous hills,
> Or swimming at night alone upon the sea,
> Whose lesser life falls from him, and the dream
> Is broken which had held him unaware,
> And with a shudder he feels his naked soul
> In the great dark world face to face with God.

[1] *Revelation and Religion*, p. 28 n.   [2] Tillich, *op. cit.* I. 276.
[3] *ib.*   [4] *Pascal's Philosophy of Religion*, p. 30.
[5] *Religious Experience*, p. 37.   [6] *op. cit.* I., pp. 228, 242, 256.

It may be that nothing so alienates not irreligious men from the claims of the Christian religion as the easy and familiar way in which some Christians speak about God, preachers alleging that God wants this, is waiting for that, is disappointed with something else, and theologians alleging their acquaintance with the inner structure of the Deity. The Transcendent as an object of worship is the personal Ground of all existence, that 'Beyond' which breaks upon our consciousness and yet utterly transcends it, the Ineffable, the Incomprehensible, so infinitely removed from us and yet in whom we with all Nature live and move and have our being.

II—VALUES

FROM Nature Rashdall infers an Universal Mind and Will, but, as he says, 'purpose is one thing; benevolent purpose is another'.[1] The argument for the goodness of God rests, not on Nature, but on our moral consciousness.[2] Our knowledge of God is not immediate but by inference; our moral reason, however, is a faculty of immediate knowledge.[3] Our moral ideals are the work of reason; they are self-evident, though not evident to all men at all stages of civilization. We have every right to assume that such truths as that the happiness of many is to be preferred to the happiness of one, that pleasure is better than pain, that goodness is of more value than pleasure, that some pleasures are better than others, hold good for God as well as for man.[4] 'In these judgements, then, we have a revelation, the only possible revelation, of the character of God'.[5]

This is a very curious list of moral ideals, but there would have been obvious inconveniences in ascribing to the character of God such of our moral ideals as courage against odds, patience under adversity, or self-control; moreover, Rashdall fully admits that the contemplation of Nature, from which we have derived our inference of the Mind and Will of God, does not suggest that the Mind behind phenomena is characterized by the Christian virtues.

On this somewhat perilous structure he raises his edifice still higher. God, it has been argued, is good and wills the good of his children; 'but when the idea of a righteous God

[1] p. 61.   [2] p. 62.   [3] p. 116.   [4] p. 62.   [5] p. 63.

34

has once been accepted, the idea of Immortality seems to me to follow from it as a sort of corollary'.[1] Conversely immortality is a postulate without which we cannot believe in God. Further, if God is good, then the evil which exists in the world must somehow be a necessary means to greater good.[2] If we speak of God as omnipotent, we must mean that he has all the power there is, and that this is the best of all possible, but not of all imaginable, universes,[3] or, as Pope argued in his Essay on Man, 'whatever is is right'.

Those of us who belonged to the privileged classes in the comfortable and tranquil and hopeful days before the 1914 war might bring ourselves to believe that this is the best of all possible worlds, for life, though beset with various hazards and disadvantages, was very satisfactory; its not intolerable evils could be accepted as in some way necessary to a further good. Rashdall's whole argument and especially its happy ending seem to us now too tidy, too easy and wholly unconvincing. Professor Karl Barth is nearer to the attitude of Christians today when he says that 'we never believe "on account of", never "because of"; we awake to faith in spite of everything'.[4] We know much less because we know much more about man and Nature than we knew in those halcyon days; the mysteries have deepened. Every expansion of our knowledge *eo ipso* enlarges our awareness of our ignorance.

'All religious truth depends logically upon inference,' says Rashdall;[5] from the contemplation of Nature we infer an Universal Mind and an Universal Will; there cannot be mind and will without some kind of feeling;[6] therefore we must infer that God is personal. Moreover from our moral consciousness which is a faculty of immediate knowledge we may infer the character of God. It is significant of the change in religious thought today that a group of Christian

[1] p. 77.   [2] p. 80.   [3] p. 85.   [4] *Dogmatics in Outline*, p. 20.
[5] p. 138.   [6] p. 45.

philosophers recently meeting to discuss the question of metaphysics were of a common mind, as Professor Ian Ramsey tells us, that 'we can no longer view natural theology as a tight, rigorous, deductive system, taking us to God by a process of unmistakable inference'.[1]

INGE ON THE REALM OF VALUES

Dean Inge's starting-point is very different. He begins with a synopsis of the outlook of Plotinus, which, he says, is closely akin to that which he will advocate:

'The nature of God, says Plotinus, is difficult to conceive and perhaps impossible to define. But we are sure of his existence because we experience, in our inmost being, expressible and definable impressions when we come near to him, or rather when he comes near to us. The ardent desire with which we turn towards him is accompanied by a pain caused by the consciousness of something lacking in ourselves; we feel that there is something wanting to our being. It must be by his presence in our souls that God reveals himself to us, for we have no means of knowing things except by something analogous to contact. The light of God's presence is brighter than the light of science or reason. But none can see it who is not made like to God, and whose being is not, like that of God, brought to an inner unity. Elsewhere, Plotinus explains faith as a kind of spiritual perception as opposed to demonstration (ἀπόδειξις), which is the result of reasoning.'[2]

It may seem a far cry from Plotinus to the people we have called 'savages' in Africa, but we may compare with Inge's summary the following passage from E. Warner's *Trial by Sasswood*: ' "Who told you what you know of God, Zabolgi?" "Told?" he repeated. "Told? Whoever is so stupid that they got to be *told* about God? Never did any

[1] *Prospect for Metaphysics*, p. 7.   [2] *Faith and its Psychology*, p. 4.

man know God from *tolds*. You get God by *feels*. All the told there is to it, is his name. You call him God; we call him Gala. I english Gala's name so you can understand me."'

In simple terms, we believe in God not as a result of logical inference but because we are aware of him. Can such a view be justified when so large a part of mankind today would confidently assert that of him they are totally unaware?

In his discussion of the traditional 'ontological' proof for the existence of God Inge says that only God himself could have put into our minds the idea of God; he adds that un-happily in mediaeval thought this consideration, which is self-explanatory, was split up into two highly controversial propositions, first that the idea of God itself implies the existence of God, and, second, that if we are aware of God, this can be only as a result of some external divine revela-tion.[1] 'According to the view which I uphold,' he writes, 'and which has been that of the best Christian philosophy from the first, there is an original, natural bond between God and the human soul.'[2]

He lays it down as a self-evident proposition that 'nothing can be proved false, if nothing is taken as true';[3] further, we can have no knowledge of anything if we can-not take as a criterion of objective truth that which it is necessary for us to think.[4] Now, we assign values to our experience, and this we do by a psychological necessity; we cannot but assign a value to a vintage port or a Rembrandt or a sunset, and even the most 'objective' of scientists is bound to speak of higher and lower forms of life. It certainly does not follow from this that all our judgements of value have objective validity, for, indeed, one man prefers beef and another mutton; *de gustibus non est disputandum*. Inge is maintaining only that, however wide of the mark our judgements of value may be, we cannot help making value judgements; 'it is impossible for the human mind to inhibit

[1] p. 182.   [2] p. 134.   [3] p. 193.   [4] p. 147.

this native propensity to assign values'.[1] We are confronted, therefore, with a realm of values as well as a realm of things.[2]

With moral and aesthetic values, he says, natural science is not concerned. He quotes Miss Benson: 'science can analyse the production of sound, and ignore the soul of music; it can show the cause of colour, and miss the joy of beauty; it can show the genesis of all manner of social institutions, and miss the heart of love; it may even find the conditions of life, but cannot ask what life is; it may sweep the heavens with its telescope, and fail to find God'. Even so, whenever the men of science speak of 'progress', of 'degeneration', of 'the survival of the *fittest*', they are making value-judgements.[3]

Indeed, the world is but 'a whirlpool of nonsense' apart from values.[4] It is with value-judgements that religion is concerned. This is the Ritschlian position. Inge's implicit criticism of Rashdall's case comes to this: we tend to regard an hypothesis as proved if by it all the relevant facts can be explained; but if we know God by inference only, then his existence is only our hypothesis. Some hypotheses, Inge agrees, are 'so inwrought with the very texture of rational experience that to deny them is to destroy experience', but even if with Rashdall we regard his proofs of the existence of a Supreme Mind and Will an hypothesis of this kind, we are at best only half-way to the God of religious faith.[5] It is through our recognition of values that we are, or may become, aware of God.

Like Rashdall Inge lays great stress upon our moral consciousness. 'The demands of our ethical nature,' he claims, 'point to the objective existence of a hierarchy of values.'[6] But he recognizes three great spheres of value, Truth, Goodness and Beauty, each of which is irreducible to the others, and these together constitute natural revela-

[1] p. 43.   [2] p. 50.   [3] pp. 43 f.   [4] Dixon, *op. cit.*, p. 339.
[5] p. 185.   [6] p. 147.

tion,[1] for these three spheres bear the marks of the transcendent or spiritual world; 'Firstly, they claim to exist in their
own right and will not be made means or instruments to
anything else, nor to each other. Secondly, they take us out
of ourselves; they are not our tools, but we are rather their
instruments. Thirdly, they are, each in its own manner and
degree, a permanent enrichment of our life—a fund of
inalienable spiritual wealth.'[2]

Inge is here meeting at a deep level the popular, superficial view that our value-judgements are mere expressions
of our desires. No doubt some of our value-judgements, as,
for instance, that cold mutton should not be eaten without
salt, are merely expressions of our personal tastes; no doubt,
too, our moral and aesthetic judgements are greatly in-
fluenced by the period and the social milieu in which our
lot is cast. Our judgements are fallible and partial. In any
particular case two good men may differ widely in their
judgement of what is the just course to pursue; we do not
know *a priori* what is just; we have to seek for justice; but
we well know, else falling short of our humanity, that the
service of Justice, so far as we can discover it, is of binding
obligation. Artists, not least at the present time, differ
widely in their judgement of what is beautiful; but to the
pursuit of Beauty every artist knows himself to be inwardly
and personally committed. The values of Truth, Goodness
and Beauty, as Inge says, are not our tools, but we are
rather their instruments. We are in touch here with the
Transcendent or, in religious terms, with God.

This is a matter of direct perception and is not capable of
proof. If any man cares to assert that to him a sunset, an
action of heroic virtue, the song of the blackbird in the
evening are occasions of pleasurable sensation or aesthetic
satisfaction merely, no argument is available for his dis-
comfort. *Aut sistitur in pulchritudine creaturæ*, says St.

[1] p. 49.   [2] p. 50.

Bonaventure, *aut per illam tenditur in aliud*;[1] in other words, we may stay within the limits of sensation, or through the sensations we may be aware of the Beyond.

> If Mary is so beautiful,
> What must her Maker be?

There are those to whom the question has no relevance. 'You never enjoy the world aright,' said Traherne, 'till the Sea itself floweth in your veins, till you are clothed with the heavens, and crowned with the stars: and perceive yourself to be the sole heir of the whole world, and more than so, because men are in it who are every one sole heirs as well as you. Till you can sing and rejoice and delight in God, as misers do in gold, and Kings in sceptres, you never enjoy the world. . . . I saw moreover that it did not so much concern us what objects were before us, as with what eyes we beheld them. All men see the same objects, but do not equally understand them.'[2]

But are not our value-judgements expressions, not of objective truth, but of our human and natural desires? To this Inge replies that 'desire does not determine truth, but truth does determine desire, and makes itself known through and as desire'.[3] *Desiderium naturale non potest esse frustra*, as Averroes put it, following Aristotle.[4] If we feel that we are being smothered, our desire for breath does not make it true that we must breathe to live, but the fact that we must breathe to live determines the desire for air. The fact that every honourable man wishes to act justly does not make his actions just, but his attempts to act justly are determined by the fact that deep in his human nature is the conviction that the claims of Justice upon him are inexorable and unqualified. Man's sense of limitless obligation to the claims of Truth, of Beauty and of Goodness is not an

---

[1] *v.* Gilson, p. 218. *The Philosophy of St. Bonaventure.*
[2] *Centuries of Meditation*, I. 29. III. 68.   [3] p. 158.
[4] *c.f.* St. Thomas, *Contra Gentiles*, III. 48.

inference from anything beyond itself; it is a direct awareness of a transcendent realm of value; it is, in religious
terms, a direct awareness of God himself.

The primary ground of faith, in Inge's view, is not
ecclesiastical authority nor even the Bible but 'the inner
personal attraction towards the good, the true and the
beautiful'.[1] Faith, then, is a response to the absolute and
transcendent values of which we become aware through the
demands of that which is revealed to us by our spiritual sen-
sibilities. It is under the three aspects of Truth, Goodness
and Beauty that we are aware of God and make response to
him.

Man does in fact pursue absolute ideals, and 'he cannot
escape from the law of his being by denying that there is an
Absolute'.[2] Moreover, 'the demands of our ethical nature
point to the objective existence of a hierarchy of values'.[3]
But, though the values somehow have objective existence,
Inge can contrast a 'world of existence' with a 'world of
values', the one consisting of brute facts and the other of our
moral, intellectual and artistic consciousness.[4] The two
worlds are never quite satisfactorily related, and while Inge
seems clearly to hold that we are aware of God or the Absolute through our moral, aesthetic and intellectual consciousness, his 'values' seem sometimes to be abstractions, less
'existent' than the world of things, and the phrase 'an
awareness of God' needs further consideration.

BEAUTY

'The essence of beauty seems to be the suitableness of
form to idea.'[5] We readers do not create the beauty of
Shakespeare's poetry; we find it there;[6] so in respect of
Nature beauty is 'a quality residing in the objects, and not

---

[1] p. 79.   [2] pp. 193 f.   [3] p. 155.   [4] p. 50.   [5] p. 48.
[6] p. 204.

imparted to them by the observer';[1] beauty, in fact, 'is a quality which the Creator has impressed, in various degrees, upon nearly all his works';[2] 'the Beautiful is essentially the Spirit making itself known sensuously';[3] we must take it therefore that 'Beauty is one of the fundamental attributes of God'.[4] Our apprehension of beauty is 'an imaginative representation which connects our present experience with the eternal. . . . The gift of imagination is thus a psychological intimation of immortality'.[5]

To define the essence of beauty as the suitableness of form to idea might seem infelicitous, if we are unable to grasp or state the idea to which the song of the nightingale, for instance, or the glory of the sunset is peculiarly suitable. Nor is it very intelligible how beauty so defined can be an attribute of God, but at least we are far advanced upon a merely intellectual conception of religion.

There will be no question that we, addicts of Beethoven or lovers of Nature, do not put the beauty into things; we find it there. But can we properly say that beauty is a quality inherent in the objects we deem beautiful?

I gaze at a work of art; I must first by a mental effort have isolated the piece of space that contains it from the rest of the space of which I am aware. I must note the colours, if it be a painting, the texture, the design; I must let the artist speak to me through the picture; the picture or the poem or the sonata is a personal communication from its creator. Pigments, canvas, lines do not speak to me; it is the artist who speaks to me through these.

I am aware of beauty in Nature; this experience comes to me through 'light-waves' and 'sound-waves' and electrical currents which set up disturbances in my brain. The beauty does not lie in light-waves or sound-waves or in electrical discharges, for I am quite unaware of them as beautiful, and if I ask the physicists what are the objects which give rise to

[1] pp. 203 f.   [2] *ib.*   [3] p. 207.   [4] p. 203.   [5] p. 2

these 'waves' and electrical discharges, they will reply in
terms of molecules and electrons which certainly do not
constitute, though they may underlie, the beauty which I
behold. It is *through* these waves and electric discharges and
molecules and electrons, but not *in* them, that I am aware
of a beauty that speaks to me. I am quite certain that I do
not create the beauty which I behold in a Bach fugue or a
sunset, nor can I quite say with Inge that beauty is a quality
residing in the objects, for the 'objects', as I understand the
scientists, are modes of energy. As in art beauty is a personal
communication from the artist somehow conveyed through
the appropriate media, it might seem natural or inevitable
to conclude that the beauty of which I am aware in Nature is a
personal communication from the Artist of the whole. I do
not draw the conclusion with Inge that beauty is a fundamental attribute of God, for to say that God is beautiful
implies that I know what God is, and this I do not know;
but my sense of the beautiful as a personal communication
and of the mystery that surrounds the physical as interpreted by modern science seems to justify the observation
of Hegel quoted by Inge: 'The Beautiful is essentially the
spiritual making itself known sensuously, presenting itself
in sensuous concrete existence, but in such a manner that
that existence is wholly and entirely permeated by the
spiritual, so that the sensuous is not independent, but has
its meaning solely and exclusively through the spiritual and
in the spiritual, and exhibits not itself but the spiritual.'[1]

We are also aware of beauties that are purely intellectual
and not sensuous. Mathematicians will agree with G. H.
Hardy in his *Mathematician's Apology* that the lure and joy
of mathematical studies is aesthetic, nor, I think, will
scientists deny that pure science is instigated and sustained
by the pursuit of beauty. Thus, says Professor Polanyi, 'to
Kepler astronomic discovery was ecstatic communion';[2] he

[1] p. 207.   [2] *Personal Knowledge*, p. 7.

speaks of 'the intellectual passions by which science appreciates its own beauty';[1] 'the affirmation of a great scientific theory is in part an expression of delight';[2] the scientist's ecstatic vision is like that of the mystics.[3] Robert Bridges puts it thus:

> While Science sitteth apart in her exile, attent
> on her other own invisibles; and working back
> to the atoms, she handleth their action to harness
> the gigantic forces of eternal motion,
> in serviceable obedience to man's mortal needs;
> and not to be interrupted nor call'd off her task,
> dreaming, amid the wonders of her sightly works,
> thru' her infinitesimals to arrive at last
> at the unsearchable immensities of Goddes realm.[4]

THE GATEWAY TO REALITY

The True, the Good and the Beautiful are our absolute values and our ideal standards. We can have no knowledge of any reality, as Hegel said, if we deny that these are manifestations of ultimate reality.[5] Thus Oman maintains that aesthetics as involving response in feeling to the form and harmony in all things is necessary for all higher knowing, [6] that sensitiveness of feeling is the only gateway to reality,[7] and that 'a true value-judgement is a judgement of reality'.[8] The whole physical medium about us may be but a system of vibrations, but the scientist interpreting these vibrations in terms of the beauty and 'simplicity' of patterns, laws and algebraic formulae may agree with the artist that 'if right values are right knowing, there is no break in principle between natural and ideal values.'[9]

'Mankind's love of life apart from the love of beauty is a

---

[1] *Personal Knowledge*, p. 134.   [2] *ib.*, p. 123.
[3] *ib.*, pp. 196 f.   [4] *op. cit.* IV., pp. 665 ff.
[5] *v.* Oman, *The Natural and the Supernatural*, p. 34.   [6] *ib.*, p. 210.
[7] *ib.*, p. 79.   [8] *ib.*, p. 203.   [9] Oman, *op. cit.*, p. 205.

tale of no count,' wrote Bridges.[1] As is wonder to the intellect, so is beauty to the soul, and beauty is the prime motive
of all men's excellence; art explores Nature for spiritual
influences, and in art material phenomena engage the soul's
depth.[2] Paul Tillich speaks of 'an immediate experience of
something ultimate in value and being of which one becomes intuitively aware'.[3] An artist or scientist may not call
himself a religious man, but there is an intimate relation
between Beauty and Religion, as Bridges puts it:

> God's worshipper
> looking on any beauty falleth straightway in love;
> and thatt love is a fire in whose devouring flames
> all earthly ills are consumed, and at least flash of it,
> be it only a faint radiancy, the freed soul glimpseth,
> nay ev'n may think to hav felt, some initiat foretaste
> of that mystic rapture, the consummation of which
> is the absorption of Selfhood in the Being of God.[4]

This approach to religion is traditionally expressed in the
'iconic' philosophy of Plato. The heart of Platonism, writes
Professor H. Armstrong, is the view that 'this world is an
image-world, a visible and changing expression of the invisible and eternal';[5] according to this view 'things are
neither valuable "in themselves" nor valueless "in themselves" but carry, simply by being what they are, a worth
and significance which is given to them from something
which is other, but not alien, which is their own proper
perfection, and more, and which remains for ever when they
pass away'. Plato's 'Ideas', he says, are to be 'identified with
God's knowledge as the exemplary cause of all things'.[6] If
in some sense the Ideas are causes, they are not merely
static.

> So if we, changing Plato's old difficult term,
> should rename his Ideas Influences, ther is none

[1] *The Testament of Beauty*, III. 748 f.
[2] *ib.* III. 795 f., I. 122, III. 1058, II. 827.
[3] *Systematic Theology*, I., p. 12.   [4] *ib.* II. 920 ff.
[5] *Prospect for Metaphysics*, p. 107.   [6] *ib.*, p. 110.

would miss his meaning nor, by nebulous logic,
wish to refute his doctrin that indeed ther are
eternal Essences that exist in themselves,
supreme efficient causes of the thoughts of men,

wrote Bridges.[1]

The tradition goes back beyond Plato. It was Pythagoras, the student of music, of poetry and of astronomy, who, as Lemprière puts it, 'considered numbers as the principles of everything, and perceived in the universe regularity, correspondence, beauty, proportion and harmony as intentionally produced by the Creator'. 'Intentionally produced by the Creator' goes beyond the argument at present, but the Greeks of the classical period were intensely aware of that beauty in the natural order of which Professor Polanyi says that it is in this scientific age the instigation, the delight, the ecstasy of scientists.

St. Bonaventure in the Platonic-Augustinian tradition takes further the conception of God as the exemplary cause of all things. Like Plato, the mathematician, he starts from number; 'number,' he says, 'is the chief exemplar in the mind of the divine Artist and also the principal footprint in creation which leads to wisdom. For the presence of number in creation is most clearly seen by all, and is also most intimate to God, making him known in all things, corporeal and sensible. Apprehending things numerical, and delighting in their proportions, we judge with certainty by the laws of these which point to God . . . Sensible things in their totality are simply shadows, echoes, symbols, footprints, images and mirrors, signs divinely given and set before us for the beholding of God, their most powerful, wise and excellent First Principle, the eternal Source and Light and Fountain of all plenitude, of all art Efficient, Exemplary and Intelligent Cause.'[2]

[1] *op. cit.* II. 834 ff.
[2] *Itinerarium Mentis in Deum*, II. 10 f. English tr. *The Franciscan Vision*, pp. 32 f.

This is a conception of religion which, I suspect, is not alien to the mysticism or reverent wonder which besets those who are truly scientists, but we must be careful to observe that it does not cover Christian dogmas.

Both Inge and Oman hold that Truth, Goodness and Beauty are reliable guides to reality,[1] but Inge held these three to be irreducible to each other, whereas Oman held that of these three the ultimate is Beauty.[2] This latter view is to be preferred. Ugliness is malformation, for everything which attains its perfection, its truth, its nature or *physis*, as the Greeks called it, is beautiful; moral goodness is the beauty of right action and right living; Beauty is therefore ultimate, and this, I suspect, is good Calvinistic doctrine too, for with Calvin the glory of God is ultimate.

AWARENESS OF GOD

But this phrase an 'awareness of God', which I have not been able to avoid, needs further elucidation especially in view of the determined claim of so many that of God they are not aware. When the sun goes behind a cloud, the birds and the wild creatures can still see, but presumably they are not aware of the sun, or, to put the matter in a more dignified and philosophical form, *ipsum quod est verum potest cognosci antequam cognoscatur ipsa veritas.*[3] We may see by the light of God, though we be not directly aware of God. 'It is evident,' says Duns, 'that something can be represented under an immutable aspect (*sub ratione immutabilis*) even if that which makes the representation is mutable in itself,' or, to revert to Oman's terminology, if God be not the Super-natural, it is through the supernatural that he is manifest.[4] The artist and the boor may

[1] Inge, *op. cit.*, p. 49; Oman, *op. cit.*, p. 213.　　[2] *op. cit.*, p. 80.
[3] 'That which is true can be recognized before Truth itself is recognized,' Duns Scotus expounding Henry of Ghent, *Op. Oxon.* I. *dist.* III. q. iv.
[4] *The Natural and the Supernatural*, p. 342.

contemplate the same field of buttercups; the same object
strikes the eye of both, but that which distinguishes the
artist's vision from the wholly inartistic man's is not a matter
of sensory perception. The artist sees in a different dimension, as it were. 'The fundamental human response to the
universe,' writes Raven, 'is an awareness of an existence
which is permanent, unitary and inclusive, which at once
welcomes and judges us, catching up into adoration and
communion and at the same time convincing us our solitari-
ness and our shame. To give expression to this experience in
appropriate cultus and creed and code is the task of the
world's religions; and the understanding, verification and
amendment of our interpretation of it is the province of
theology."[1]

> That there is beauty in natur and that man loveth it
> are one thing and the same; neither can be derived
> apart as cause of the other.[2]

In order to make as plain as is within the capacity of
words what I mean by 'awareness of God' I have cited
those who speak in very varied idioms. Let one more illustration be accepted:

> For giving me desire
> An eager thirst, a burning ardent fire,
> A virgin infant flame,
> A love with which into the world I came,
> An inward, hidden, heavenly love
> Which in my soul doth work and move,
> And ever ever me inflame
> With restless longing, heavenly avarice,
> That never could be satisfied,
> That did incessantly a Paradise
> Unknown suggest, and something undescried
> Discern, and bear me to it; be
> Thy Name for ever praised by me.[3]

---

[1] *Experience and Interpretation*, p. 185.
[2] *The Testament of Beauty*, III. 783 f.   [3] Traherne, *Desire.*

John Baillie, therefore, is right to claim that faith is a mode of primary apprehension; it is 'at the same time a mode of apprehension and a mode of active response to that apprehension'.[1] An awareness of God cannot be proved; it can only be experienced.

THE EXISTENCE OF GOD SELF-EVIDENT

Man is, or may be, aware of the Transcendent through the values of Truth, of Beauty and of Goodness, but this contention falls short of Inge's claim, following Plotinus and Anselm, that there is 'an original, natural bond between God and the human soul'.[2] By the structure of his nature man desires knowledge, as is shewn in his innate curiosity; second, he desires happiness, for *omnia bonum appetunt*, all things aim at the good; man is often misled as to what is truly good, but no man acts except to achieve some good in the achievement of which he will find happiness; third, man seeks for peace in the satisfaction of his desire for knowledge and for the good wherein lies happiness. But curiosity or the love of knowledge knows no limits nor can find satisfaction in any finite object; again, our desire for the good, wherein lies our happiness, is boundless nor can it be limited to any finite object; our peace, therefore, also points us to the infinite. Therefore *nata est anima ad percipiendum bonum infinitum, quod Deus est, ideo in eo solo debet quiescere et eo frui*.[3] We must maintain, then, not merely that some men *may be* aware of the Transcendent through the values of Truth, of Goodness and of Beauty, but also that *all* men by their very nature are directed towards that infinite Good which we call God. The reality of God is self-evident, though not all men see it.

---

[1] *The Sense of the Presence of God*, pp. 66, 90.   [2] *supra*, p. 137.
[3] Bonaventure, *I. Sent* 1.3.2. v. Gilson, *The Philosophy of St. Bonaventure*, pp. 87–89, 'the soul is born for the perception of an infinite good, which is God; therein alone, therefore, must it rest and find enjoyment'.

This is really the contention of St. Anselm in the *Proslogion*, which is unhappily styled 'the ontological proof' of God's existence. St. Anselm argues that God, who is that than which no greater can be conceived, must exist, for if, so to put it, he did not exist, a greater, namely, an existent, could be conceived, and this would be God. The argument has seemed abstract and unconvincing; it is justified by C. C. J. Webb, St. Anselm's translator, as being the assertion that thought is the criterion of reality.[1] Kant is generally supposed to have disposed of St. Anselm once for all by observing that there is a wide difference between the idea of a hundred dollars and a hundred dollars in the pocket; the actual existence of God cannot be deduced from the bare idea of God. But this is to misunderstand St. Anselm who is here concerned not with physical objects but with values. Through the values of Truth, of Goodness and of Beauty we are aware of a transcendent *reality*; we are aware of many perfections; the sum and ground of all perfections is God, the Absolute Reality. This, once you see it, is self-evident. If through values we are in touch with *reality*, then God is.

Dr. Franks has pointed out that, though both St. Thomas and Kant repudiated the argument of St. Anselm, each in his own way has restated it. St. Thomas, starting, as he supposed, from things or sensible experience, claims to prove that essence and existence are one in God. That is St. Anselm's contention in another form. Moreover, St. Thomas did not start in fact from bare sensible experience, but also from an awareness of the mutability, the contingency, the relativity of all things sensible, which itself presupposes a logically prior sense of the immutable, the necessary and the absolute; 'our experience of God's existence is the very condition of the inference by which we claim to establish that God exists'.[2] In respect of Kant Dr. Franks has argued that

[1] *The Devotions of St. Anselm*, p. 51.   [2] Gilson, *op. cit.*, p. 125.

in his proof that there is Good Will at the heart of things Kant 'has founded a new metaphysic or, rather, has established the old metaphysic of Anselm and Aquinas upon new lines'.[1] St. Bonaventure's saying, *aliquo posito ponitur verum, et vero posito ponitur veritas quae est causa omnis veri,* is thus expounded by Gilson, 'each particular truth implies the existence of an absolute truth whereof it is the effect. Therefore to affirm any individual truth at all is to affirm the existence of God. . . . If something is true, then the first Truth exists. Therefore one cannot deny the existence of truth or the existence of God without in that very act affirming the thing denied'.[2] We seem here to be trenching upon the theme of our next chapter, but how nearly this argument is concerned with values appears from John Baillie's parallel statement, 'even when it is our friend whom we trust, our trust is ultimately in the ground of all being'.[3]

---

[1] *The Atonement*, p. 115, *c.f.* the whole chapter on the 'Outline of a Metaphysic of Christianity'.
[2] *op. cit.*, p. 131.   [3] *op. cit.*, p. 39.

III—RELIGION AND TRUTH

BEFORE we turn to Christianity, which is our proper subject, it will be well to consider more closely what we should mean by the word 'religion' or at least what is intended by it in these pages, and, second, what is the nature of religious knowledge, if, indeed, religious knowledge is possible for man while still *in statu viatoris*, on his pilgrim way.

CONSCIOUSNESS AND THE MECHANICAL ASPECT OF THE WORLD

If knowledge is to be possible for us at all, we must suppose that 'reality will not deceive us, if we approach it with the right questions, and if, in sincerity, we spare no pains to understand its answers'.[1] I have no means of proving that the material world exists except that I am aware of it; I have no means of proving that my friends exist except only that I am aware of them; 'we cannot prove the reality of any environment while omitting the only evidence it ever gives of itself, which is the way in which it environs us'.[2] But in truth we are only aware of our own existence in our awareness of other persons and of things.[3] Inge speaks of a 'realm of existence' and a 'realm of values'; this is unhappy, for it suggests that whereas the material world is there 'objectively' for all to see, the realm of values consists of our personal and 'subjective' estimate of objects.

The physicists lead us to think that the physical world about us may ultimately be reduced to an ordered system

[1] Oman, *The Natural and the Supernatural*, p. 100.
[2] Oman, *op. cit.*, p. 52.
[3] *v.* J. MacMurray, *The Self as Agent, passim.*

of vibration. But the mechanical aspect of the world cannot be the whole of its reality, for, as Oman says, 'from pure mechanical vibration without meaning there is no possible opening into knowing, which is all meaning'.[1] Not only does a personal coefficient shape all factual knowledge,[2] but when I contemplate a rainbow, the reality of the rainbow is not the vibrations nor the raindrops but the colours. Even the reckoning of vibrations is a mental judgement of valuation, not a mere transcript of events, and all our judgements are value-judgements concerned with usefulness or significance or worth.

It is a very naïve view 'that we can know the mechanical physical series to be real, while we regard the consciousness by which we know as a mere effect of a cause which may have no resemblance to it'.[3] 'While I have been speaking, and in order to express my thought,' said H. W. B. Joseph in his lecture on the Concept of Evolution, 'there have been various movements of my organs of speech. If these movements are to be wholly accounted for by reference to the state of my cerebral centres, and other bodily parts, and that state by reference to previous dispositions of what is material, my thought has had nothing to do with my speech.' To say that my speech, a physical vibration intrinsically meaningless, is real while my thought, which is all meaning, is unreal seems curious nonsense. If existence is correlative to knowability, it is a contradiction to say that the physical aspect of things alone is real, for 'real' is a mental judgement of significance, and 'things' cannot be more real than the knower presupposed in their existence.[4]

A SUPER-NATURAL ENVIRONMENT

As human beings we are aware of external things, of

[1] *op. cit.*, p. 158.   [2] M. Polanyi, *Personal Knowledge*, p. 17.
[3] Oman, *op. cit.*, pp. 34 f.   [4] *v. supra*, p. 19.

ourselves as conscious beings, of our friends, of beauty in nature and art, of obligations of loyalty and duty. Our human environment is twofold; it is partly visible and partly invisible, or partly material and partly spiritual, or, to use Oman's language, it is partly natural and partly super-natural. It would be misleading, however, to say that the men of science are concerned only with our natural or physical environment while religion is solely concerned with our super-natural or spiritual environment, for, if applied science busies itself with the use of our material environment, pure science with mathematics is concerned with pattern and with beauty, with order and with wonder. Religion is concerned with our unseen environment, but, as Oman says, 'the really important mark of a religion is its attitude to the natural'.[1] As man's applied science is his response, or part of his response, to the physical aspect of his environment, so religion is his response, or part of his response, to the unseen or spiritual aspect of his environment. Schleiermacher is misinterpreted when he is understood to reduce religion to mere feeling. When he defined religion as 'the feeling of absolute dependence', he meant by feeling, says Tillich, 'the immediate awareness of something unconditional'.[2] True or right religion is a right relation to the ultimate reality, whether this be as for Kant the moral order, or the artistic harmony of the universe as for Schleiermacher, or the cosmic process of reason as for Hegel. All these alike regarded the ultimate reality as absolute in its claim, religion as the recognition of this claim and therein as emancipation from bondage to the sensible, the transient and the accidental.[3]

Religion, then, is to be defined as man's response to his spiritual or immaterial or super-natural environment, through which he apprehends that which is ultimate, abso-

---

[1] *op. cit.*, p. 364.   [2] *Systematic Theology*, p. 47.
[3] Oman, *op. cit.* p. 28.

lute and unchanging. That man's sense of what is ultimate and unconditional and absolute may be dim, imperfect or even grotesque is evident enough, but even the primitive 'savage' who regards his absurd fetish as a thing of immeasurable wonder, and who holds the rules of taboo to be of binding and unconditional obligation, is aware of a supernatural environment, of an absolute or an 'ought' that is an unconditional imperative. Only gradually does man come to recognize that which alone deserves his utmost reverence or lays upon him truly unconditional obligation. It is in the light of these principles that the history of religions and, indeed, of civilizations can most profitably be assessed. The old notion that Christianity as declared by its prophets and administered by its officials is the one true religion, and that all other religions, so-called, are of demonic inspiration, will not hold, for all religion is man's fumbling response to his super-natural environment. Empirical Christianity falls under this condemnation of fumbling like any other faith; it is one religion among many. True religion will be man's right relationship to his super-natural environment. If this right relationship is to be seen in the Founder of Christianity, it is very imperfectly to be discovered in most of those who have come after him.

Truth lies in contact with reality. A tone-deaf or blind man through his infirmity misses an important contact with his physical environment; a man wholly without sense of moral obligation, if such there be, would be unaware of a great part of man's spiritual or super-natural environment,

'and beauty dead, black Chaos comes again'.

Human experience offers us no reason to suppose that the non-material element in our environment is less 'real' than the physical, that while Einstein has something of importance to say to us, Mozart has nothing, that 'facts' can be isolated from their significance. We are as conscious of the spiritual or non-material influences that surround us as we are of physical existences, though, emerging as we are but slowly from the animal state to the fully human state, we have more consensus of opinion about 'things' than about significance or meaning. The cultural or spiritual advance of man would have been impossible were not the spiritual or super-natural his environment, nor would the super-natural have challenged him had he not by nature already belonged to it. The history of religion is 'a long endeavour to know a higher environment by learning to live rightly in it'.[1] The knowledge of how to adapt ourselves rightly to our physical environment is, in large measure, part of our inheritance from the animal kingdom; rightly to adapt ourselves to our spiritual environment is the new and exacting task of human nature.

The denial of the super-natural is a commonplace of Marxist philosophy as of the current rationalism of the West; for this reason Oman's use of the term 'super-natural', which I have always written with a hyphen, may be misleading, but Communists and secularists are aware, as are other men, of those non-material or spiritual influences which play upon us through music or the plastic arts or the contemplation of natural beauty or the claims of obligation and affection; not for nothing was Karl Marx called 'the last of the Hebrew prophets', and the Communist Manifesto rings with moral passion. As Dr. Polanyi observes, if Marxism really sought material values only, it would lose its fanaticism; Marx purports to treat moral sentiments as hypocrisy; he hides his moral indignation under the disguise of a scientific statement.[2] I was recently introduced to a distinguished physicist who had declared that he believed nothing which he could not measure. I soon found that he is married to a delightful lady whom he loves and trusts! To such ridiculous inconsistencies and contra-

[1] Oman, *op. cit.*, p. 355. [2] *op. cit.*, pp. 232 f.

dictions are they prone who express their disbelief in spiritual values. The crude materialist claims that all our mental life is but epiphenomenon, a mist or cloud, as it were, thrown off by brains; to the Buddhist or Vedantist, on the other hand, all the material series is unreal; there is no proving the reality of a material world or of a spiritual world except that, if we are honest with our experience, we are aware of both.

THE RELIGIOUS ASPECT OF EXPERIENCE

Every event has many aspects. To put a voting paper in the ballot-box is an action that may be differently treated by the chemist, the physicist, the psychologist, the sociologist, the artist, the politician and the moralist; while all these treat, each after his kind, with the same event, it seems foolish to suppose that some are dealing with real aspects and others with unreal. If we may disregard the claims made for ecstatic mysticism, we may say that the super-natural always comes to us through, and not apart from, the material and natural. The super-natural is embodied in the natural. 'Nothing,' says Tillich,' is essentially and inescapably secular.'[1] Our task is to make the natural or physical 'diaphanous for the spiritual'.[2]

Blake is reported to have said that 'if the door of perception were cleansed, everything would appear to man as it is —infinite'. Perception, in fact, is hindered by explanation and by all the accompanying memories and ideas which we adults unconsciously associate with our perceptions. It is artists and poets and pre-eminently children whose awareness and apprehension are clearest and most undimmed. Children, writes Joyce Cary, 'feel everything in life directly, without analysis or reason'.[3] If, therefore, we would seek

[1] *op. cit.* I., p. 242.   [2] Oman, *op. cit.*, p. 338.
[3] *A House of Children*, p. 64.

light upon our sensible environment, it is to them rather
than to philosophers and scientists that we should turn.

The primary mark of religion is a sense of the sacred
which involves a judgement of absolute valuation, that this
or that ideal or action or beauty is of incommensurable
worth, that this or that obligation lays upon us an unconditional demand. The judgement of the sacred 'makes a
quite different demand from any claim of profit or con-
venience'.[1] Men have derided religion as mere mass-feeling
or herd-instinct, but it is precisely religion or the sense of
the sacred that has enabled man to say No to the demands of
society or the traditions of the past.

When we deal with religion, we are not in the field of
proof or demonstration. If a man have no ear for music, you
can discuss with him the mathematics of harmony, but it is
impossible to prove to him the majesty of Beethoven's great
compositions. If a man does not see that cruelty is wrong,
you cannot profitably hope to demonstrate his error. If a
man declare himself an atheist, you cannot by any expertise
of logic prove that he is mistaken; but in this last case, if he
be a man of moral and spiritual and aesthetic sensibility,
you may perhaps be able to persuade him that he is aware
of the Transcendent and the Unconditional though hitherto
he has not called this by the name of God.

As we grow up and enrich our experience, we learn to
feel our way into the world of art or of science or of religion.
All that may be required of us is seriousness of purpose and
an honest mind open to all that our environment would
teach us. For a scientist to close his eyes to any facts or to
seek to impose his preconceived theories upon the facts is a
kind of treason. Religion is an aspect of the human spirit of
wider range than science, for it concerns life at every point;
here, too, we should likewise be guilty of the same kind of
treason if, in the interests of conformity with our ecclesias-

[1] Oman, *op. cit.*, p. 55.

tical or, it may be, our anti-ecclesiastical traditions or in the interests of peace of mind or 'spiritual comfort', we should close our minds to anything that our super-natural or spiritual or non-material environment should be teaching us, or claim to impose our dogmatic or our antidogmatic theories upon reality. To this the men of science will readily agree. Christians and anti-Christians often lack the scientific conscience and thereby close their minds to truth.

We must be honest with, and open to, the world which is our environment alike in its physical and its meta-physical or immaterial or spiritual or super-natural aspects. It is by no accident that 'births, deaths and marriages' constitute an epitome of our human life, by no accident that so much of our poetry, so many of our popular songs and the stories we read are concerned with the love of man and maid. The reason is that the experience of 'falling in love' is one of the chief occasions, and perhaps for many almost the sole occasion, when they are transported by a sense of wonder, of mystery, of the transcendent and the absolute. To many this strange sense of awe and wonder returns when they look upon their first-born child; to many it recurs as they stand by the graveside of one whom they have loved or honoured. But all men of moral or aesthetic sensibility are conscious from time to time of a moral demand or of a beauty which points to something ultimate. When we read of some heroic action which wins a posthumous V.C., we think of it not as a folly but as a magnificence; even to the botanist in his most scientific mood 'a primrose by the river's brim' is more than just *primula vulgaris*; it is a mystery of wonder and of beauty. It would be mental and personal dishonesty to deny our spiritual or immaterial or super-natural environment, interpreting it as an exhalation of our fancy.

So far we may say no more than this, that we are aware of a realm of things (or of vibrations, if that be the last word of

science) and a realm of the spirit, an awareness through the
physical and transient of the transcendent and the absolute.
If we divide reality into the personal and the impersonal,
we must say that the world of things is the world of the impersonal, and the world of the spirit is in some way, however
obscure, a personal world of meaning and communication.

Dr. H. H. Farmer in his Gifford Lectures finds a
'normative concept of religion' in the Christian revelation
and experience. He recognizes seven moments in the apprehension of God; in the Christian religion properly understood, he holds, these seven moments are in harmony and
balance, and he suggests that where any of them is absent
at least in nuance there religion is really absent. His seven
'moments' as I call them, are these: (1) An apprehension
of God as 'the ultimate source of all being, the one self-
subsistent underived Reality'; (2) an apprehension of God
'as being in himself the realized perfection of all value'; (3)
an apprehension of God as personal; (4) an apprehension of
him as making an absolute claim upon the worshipper; (5)
an apprehension of him 'as the final succour and security of
man's life'; (6) an apprehension of a personal God as the
inward source of the worshipper's life and power; (7) a
feeling-tone akin to awe 'which accompanies and, is appropriate to, the living encounter with *God*'.[1]

Dr. Farmer, we may say, has analysed the religious
experience at its highest, and by this norm appraises all the
manifold religious or apparently religious phenomena of
human history. I have approached the subject from the
other end, sharing the view expressed by John Baillie in
Our Knowledge of God that all men are aware of God,
though many do not realize that it is of God that they are
aware. I should claim, for instance, that an atheist's sense of
unconditional obligation *is* an awareness of the Transcendent, that any response to the Transcendent is religious or

[1] *Revelation and Religion*, pp. 78 f.

antireligious, and that the Transcendent manifests itself to us in such a way that it must be spoken of in personal rather than impersonal terms. Dr. Farmer may well be right that where an awareness of the Transcendent actually becomes a consciously religious attitude, all those moments which he has enumerated and analysed so carefully and fruitfully are present at least in embryo or by implication. But there can be, I think, an unconsciously religious attitude. I should again cite in evidence the response of the ordinary man to those deeds which win the posthumous award of the Victoria Cross. For if there be no Beyond, no world of spiritual realities at least as 'real' as our physical environment, these actions are often frankly silly and without justification in philosophy or common sense. If there be no world invisible about us, heroic actions are the foolish risking or throwing away of valuable lives; it is moreover a waste of time to listen to Bach; and Turner must be regarded as a mere distortionist of Nature.

By religion, then, I am meaning response to our non-physical or spiritual or super-natural environment. And since we could not know our natural or physical environment unless it made itself known to us through our senses, so we could not know our spiritual environment unless it made itself known to us through our 'sense of beauty' or our 'sense of obligation' or our 'sense of awe'. It is customary to retain the word 'revelation' for the self-manifestation of the spiritual world, but the term, which means an unveiling of that which was there while we were unaware of it, is equally applicable in both cases.

THE NATURE OF KNOWING

We have knowledge of the physical world. Can we be said to have knowledge of the non-physical or spiritual world?

I should venture to criticize much or even most of the

post-Reformation theology, especially such as purports simply to expound 'the Biblical revelation', on the ground that it has no clear epistemological foundation. The writers do not make clear what they mean by knowing. A theology unconnected with an explicit epistemology hangs in the air. I am sure that the Thomist distinction, generally accepted by Protestants also, between 'truths of reason' and 'truths of revelation' must be abandoned, and that we must revert to the Augustinian–Franciscan tradition, that all knowing is of one kind, and that all knowledge is in the last resort an apprehension of, or rather a participation in, the Ultimate Reality which is God. All knowledge comes by illumination of the mind, and all our illumination is, as St. Augustine put it, 'a participation in the Word'.[1]

One man will say, 'I know that it will rain this afternoon,' another, 'I know that Harold was killed at the Battle of Hastings,' a third, 'I know that the earth revolves round the sun,' and Job said 'I know that my Redeemer liveth'. In these sentences is the verb 'to know' used in the same sense or in quite different senses, and, in particular, how could Job possibly know that his Redeemer liveth?

First, knowledge is a kind of possession or of union. When a man knows something, then, to use spatial metaphors, that which was outside his mind, the thing known, is mirrored within his mind by the correct idea; he has the thing known, as we say, 'in his mind', he possesses it in the form of knowledge; or we may say, if we prefer, that the thing known exists in two modes, first as it is outside his mind, and, second, as it is in his mind. Truth, says Polanyi, is 'the rightness of mental acceptance'.[2] Truth, as the Schoolmen said, is an *adaequatio intellectus et rei*, an equation of the mind and the thing. Better, 'knowing', as

[1] *Illuminatio nostra . . . participatio Verbi. De Trin.*, IV. 4.ii. See further the chapter *de Veritate* in my book *The Abyss of Truth*, reprinted now in *The Place of Understanding and Other Papers*.
[2] *op. cit.*, p. 321.

Tillich says following Aristotle, 'is a form of union'.[1] 'The actualities of the sensible object and of the sensitive faculty,' Aristotle had said, 'are *one* actuality in spite of the difference between their modes of being', 'actual knowledge is identical with its object', and 'the soul is in a way all existing things; for existing things are either sensible or thinkable'.[2]

Second, all knowing is in terms of meaning or significance. If I say that I know what a chair is, or I know the chair upon which I am sitting now, I am thinking of something of a certain shape that is resistant to pressure and that is constructed to be sat upon. My knowledge, then, is at every point relevant to its meaning for me. If besides being a man who needs at times to sit I am also a physicist and can think of a chair in terms of protons, neutrons and electrons, I am still thinking in terms that are relative to mind and therefore to meaning even if not to sensible experience. Many things are unknown to us, but if, to use an Irishism, there were anything that were intrinsically unknowable—unknowable, that is, not merely to the human mind but to mind as such or to the Universal Mind—that thing could not be said to exist, or to say that it existed would be meaningless; existence and knowability are correlative terms. The human mind can only apprehend that which is in some way relative to human experience and human life, and all knowledge is in terms of meaning or significance. If we can know God at all, it can only be as embodied human beings can know him; we cannot know him as, perhaps, angels or skylarks know him.

Third, into all knowledge there enters a personal equation. Polanyi has insisted upon this in respect of scientific knowledge. After pointing out that there have been three stages in the development of modern physical sciences, first, belief in a system of number and of geometrical patterns, second, belief in mechanically controlled masses,

[1] *op. cit.* I. 105.   [2] *de Anima*, III. 426a; III. 430a; III. 429a.

and, third, belief in a system of mathematical invariances (for today, as Bridges wrote, 'Mathematick rideth as a queen'),[1] he urges that scientific knowledge is not impersonal, that science 'is a system of beliefs to which we are committed, and which therefore cannot be represented in non-committal terms', that 'no intelligence, however critical or original, can operate outside . . . a fiduciary framework', and that into every act of knowing there enters a tacit and passionate contribution of the person knowing'.[2] What we know and cannot prove, he says, underlies all we can prove'.[3] In fact, we know, at least in part, by faith.

If this personal equation is present in all scientific knowledge, it is more obviously so in all moral and aesthetic knowledge. Some urge that here we are dealing with convention or taste but not with knowledge, and there is no doubt that our ideas of right and wrong are largely conventional, and that our aesthetic judgements are modified by our tastes, but the principle that matters of morals and aesthetics are solely concerned with convention and taste is a dishonest judgement in the sense that it is a theory imposed upon our experience and not given to us in experience. Rationalism, says Oman, is 'a protection against the appeal and challenge of all experience'.[4] We must follow Oman in the view that 'knowledge is right meaning in our minds by active interpretation of a meaning that is the true reality', and thus the gift of seeing colour is in comparison with the lot of one who is colour blind 'a higher way of perceiving and not merely a higher way of being pleased'.[5]

Knowledge is an apprehension of reality in terms of meaning or significance. It is a fiduciary act in the sense that it involves a personal response. Truth, Beauty, Justice are not 'facts'; they can only be apprehended as we serve them.[6]

---

[1] *op. cit.*, IV. 857.   [2] *op. cit.*, pp. 164, 169, 171, 266, 312.
[3] *ib.*, p. 286.   [4] *op. cit.*, p. 322.   [5] *op. cit.*, pp. 201 f.
[6] *v.* Polanyi, *op. cit.*, p. 279.

Religious knowledge is not other except in its frame of reference. Oman speaks of faith as a divine endowment of our nature prompting us to look for a meaning in life.[1] Every judgement expresses an insight into meaning or significance either for the senses or for man's spiritual or intellectual life. All discovery is revelation; the two words bear one meaning; the first points to the uncovering of that which was hidden, the second to the unveiling of that which lay concealed. We cannot prove the existence of God; yet, as Tillich argues, reason itself raises the question of revelation.[2]

How can we know God? God cannot be an 'object', for, as Tillich says, he precedes the subject-object structure, and infinity is not a thing but a demand.[3] He therefore distinguishes between 'technical' and 'ontological' reason. By the technical reason we can manipulate the world, by the ontological reason is meant 'the structure of the mind which enables it to grasp and to shape reality'.[4] He also distinguishes subjective from objective reason; 'subjective reason is the rational structure of the mind, while objective reason is the rational structure of reality'; the *logos* or reason within us grasps reality, because reality itself has a *logos* character.[5] Philosophy, he says, deals theoretically with the structure of being; religion deals existentially with its meaning.[6]

Reason is much more than reasoning. By reasoning we mean ratiocination, the ability whereby the mind proceeds by argument from point to point. But it is by reason, not by reasoning, that we apprehend those first principles upon which all reasoning must rest. It is by reason, for instance, that we apprehend that the same proposition cannot be at once true and false at the same time and in the same respect;

[1] *op. cit.*, p. 223.   [2] *op. cit.* I., p. 90.   [3] *ib.* I., pp. 191, 212.
[4] *op. cit.* I., pp. 80, 83.   [5] *op. cit.* I., pp. 86, 83.
[6] *op. cit.* I., p. 254.

it is by reason that we apprehend truth, goodness, beauty and 'the fundamental lines that are driven through the universe in the endeavour to map it out and understand its inner relations'.[1]

We cannot prove the existence of God by reasoning, but if we have any apprehension of the divine, it can only be by the faculty of reason. Yet how shall the finite be *capax infiniti*, able to apprehend the infinite? We cannot answer that question; only God could give us the thought of God, but we are, at least at times, aware of the Infinite, the Absolute, the Sacred, the Divine by what Tillich calls a certain 'ecstasy' of the reason. Ecstasy, he says, is a state of mind, in which reason is beyond itself; 'revelation is the manifestation of the depth of reason and the ground of being. It points to the mystery of existence and to our ultimate concern'; 'ecstasy is the miracle of the mind and that miracle is the ecstasy of reality'.[2]

REVELATION

That ecstasy of the mind is described or indicated in classical form in the passage of St. Augustine's *Confessions* in which he describes his conversation with his mother shortly before her death when 'she and I were leaning by ourselves on the ledge of a window, from which we looked down on the garden of our house. Yonder it was, in Ostia by Tiber, where, away from the crowd, fatigued by the long journey from Milan, we were recruiting ourselves for the sea voyage. Sweet was the converse we held together, as, forgetting those things that were behind, and reaching forth unto those things which were before, we asked ourselves in the presence of thee, the Truth, what will be the manner of that eternal life of the saints, which eye hath not seen, nor ear heard, neither hath it entered into the heart of man.

[1] R. S. Franks, *The Atonement*, p. 101.   [2] *op. cit.* I. 124, 130 f.

With the lips of our souls we panted for the heavenly streams of thy fountain, the fountain of life which is in thee, that, sprinkled with that water to the measure of our capacity, we might attain some poor conception of that glorious theme. And as our converse drew to this conclusion, that the sweetest conceivable delight of sense in the brightest conceivable earthly sunshine was not to be compared, no, nor even named, with the happiness of that life, we soared with glowing hearts towards the same, mounting step by step the ladder of the material order, through heaven itself, whence sun and moon and stars shed their radiance upon the earth. And still higher did we climb by the staircase of the spirit, thinking and speaking of thee, and marvelling at thy works. And so we came to our own minds, and passed beyond them into the region of unfailing plenty, where thou feedest Israel for ever with the food of truth, where Life is Wisdom by which all these things come to be, both the things that have been and the things which shall be; and the Life itself never comes to be, but is, as it was and shall be evermore, because in it is neither past nor future but present only, for it is eternal; for past and future are not eternal. *And as we talked and yearned after it, we touched it for an instant with the whole force of our hearts*'.[1] It may be thought that all men of spiritual sensitivity will have had some experience which enables them to understand what St. Augustine means.

Revelation, says Tillich, is 'the manifestation of the ground of being for human knowledge'; it is 'the manifestation of the depth of reason and the ground of being'; the phrase 'natural revelation' he deems almost a contradiction, for as natural knowledge it is not revelation; 'revelation is the manifestation of the mystery of being to the cognitive function of human reason'.[2] There is nothing that cannot

---

[1] IX. 10, Bigg's translation, my italics.
[2] *op. cit.* I., pp. 105, 130 f., 133, 143.

enter into a revelatory correlation; that is to say, the mystery
of being may dawn upon the mind of a man through any
object or event, and 'knowledge of revelation cannot inter-
fere with ordinary knowledge', nor is knowledge of revelation exposed to critical analysis by scientific or historical
research.[1] Revelation is not information; it is an awareness
of God as the Ground of all being. Music, poetry, painting
and the arts, says Polanyi, lie somewhere between science
and worship.[2]

If it is through the finite that we may become aware of the
infinite, through the changing of the changeless, theology
is concerned with experience and is no substitute for it, nor
is faith independent of intellectual processes. 'We know our
environment,' says Oman, 'only as we live rightly in it,' and,
at least for those who have eyes to see, 'the reality of the
evanescent is the revelation of things eternal as the spirit's
inalienable and abiding possession'.[3]

Revelation is not information; it is a glimpse of the glory
of God and as such is inevitably ineffable. What then is the
place of dogma in religion? To this we shall come later. At
the moment it must suffice to animadvert upon the language
of religion.

Theological statements about God are sometimes taken
by theologians and even more frequently by non-theologians
as in intention literally true. Literally true they cannot be.
The Being of God is incomprehensible to mortal men. This
does not mean that silence is imposed upon us. That which
we have seen we must declare, but all our language here can
be but metaphorical, analogical or symbolic. Its truth is not
like the accuracy of scientific definition; if it is true, it has
the profounder truth of poetry.

> O, my Luve's like a red red rose
> That's newly sprung in June:

---

[1] *op. cit.*, pp. 131, 144.   [2] *op. cit.*, p. 199.
[3] *op. cit.*, pp. 456, 465.

O, my Luve's like the melodie
That's sweetly played in tune.

You cannot put that into prose. The poet is expressing a
vision or truth which not all the chemists and physiologists
and psychologists and moralists and sociologists and theologians together could express with comparable exactitude.
The poet is declaring the truth of his vision as only a poet
can, but what he says is not literally true. Another poet has
a vision; he writes a sonnet to express, as well as words can,
that which he has seen; then the commentators and literary
critics get to work upon his composition. I once asked Dr.
Martin Buber whether he thought he knew the meaning of
the divine name, which we have englished as Jehovah, in
the Bible. Whether he would stand by his answer, whether
he meant me to take it literally, I do not know. Ya or Yahu
was, he said, the original form; 'hu' is the Hebrew for 'he'
in English. 'Ya—it is he! it is he!'—that is the meaning of
the name. This corresponds to the poet's vision. Then he
may go on to say 'he is the Lord', 'he is the Shepherd of
Israel', 'he is the Lord of hosts' and so forth; this corresponds to the poet's sonnet. Finally there are the many
theologies of the Old Testament, which correspond with the
work of commentators and of critics.

'Ya—it is he! it is he!'—we may compare Gandhi's last
words when he was dying, 'He, Ram! He, Ram!' (Ah,
God! Ah, God!). It is told of St. Francis of Assissi that,
rising from bed when he supposed his companion to be
asleep, he spent hours in prayer, but his only words were
'My God! My God!'. Theology is two very long steps from
revelation, and the intermediate step of symbol is but the
stammering of the soul to express the inexpressible.

INTERMEZZO

THE preceding argument may be summarized in this
fashion: Nature or the universe as we apprehend it directly
through our senses or indirectly by the conclusions and
hypotheses to which scientific investigations point, is a
series of inter-connected patterns of unimaginable range
and complication. That all this occurs by chance is in itself
inconceivable, as it is inconceivable that rational creatures
should emerge from a universe that is itself irrational.
Pattern is correlative to intention or intelligence, and we
are driven to the conclusion that the universe is in some way,
utterly obscure to us, the product of Intelligence. This
material world (for so we call it, though we cannot say what
'matter' is) at last produces life and ultimately man who
with his reason is able to study and to contemplate that
whole of which he is an emergent part; the intelligence in
man recognizes the Intelligence in the whole or the rational
pattern that the universe presents. Nature, we may say,
comes to self-consciousness in man. But man does more
than recognize pattern; by a necessity of his being he
ascribes values, and value is correlative to meaning; he has
awarenesses that are not given in sensible perception; it is
not apart from his senses but it is not through his senses,
that he is aware of virtue, of beauty or the claims of truth.
Moreover, his judgement of Nature as transient and imperfect is not logically intelligible unless he has *a priori* or 'at
the back of his mind', as we say, the notion of the eternal
and the perfect. The animals, so far as we know, take life as
it comes; they are aware of change, but not of transience,
of suffering but not of imperfection. Man is aware, in fact,

of a double environment, a physical, material sensible or natural environment and a non-physical, immaterial, spiritual or super-natural environment. He is aware of the latter through the former.

Oman speaks of a natural and a super-natural environment. Simone Weil speaks rather of the reality of this world and the reality that lies beyond this world. 'There is,' she says, 'a reality outside the world, that is to say, outside space and time, outside man's mental universe, outside any sphere whatsoever that is accessible to human faculties. Corresponding to this reality, at the centre of the human heart, is the longing for an absolute good, a longing which is always there and is never appeased by any object in this world. Another terrestrial manifestation of this reality lies in the absurd and insoluble contradictions which are always the terminus of human thought when it moves exclusively in this world. Just as the reality of this world is the sole foundation of facts, so that other reality is the sole foundation of good. That reality is the unique source of all the good that can exist in this world: that is to say, all beauty, all truth, all justice, all legitimacy, all order and all human behaviour that is mindful of obligations. . . . Although it is beyond the reach of any human faculties, man has the power of turning his attention and love towards it.'[1]

Ultimately we have not two environments but one environment with two aspects, which we distinguish as the spiritual and the material; we have to do not with two realities, this world and the world beyond, but with one Reality and with phenomena or appearances; the degree of 'reality' which inheres in phenomena we cannot tell, for the ultimate nature of 'matter' is to us insoluble mystery at present. For our immediate purposes it is enough to recognize that there is a spiritual or super-natural

[1] From the Profession of Faith which introduces her Draft for a Statement of Human Obligations, *Selected Essays*, 1934–1943, p. 219.

environment which is constantly impinging upon our consciousness, there is a spiritual reality outside ourselves and beyond this world of sense.

A man's religion or, it may be, his anti-religion is his attitude to this spiritual environment, this reality beyond the world of sense. Duty, we say, makes demands upon us, beauty makes appeal to us, the claims of loyalty are binding on us; there is a longing within us for that which no finite thing can satisfy. We are aware of the Transcendent, in fact, as in some sense personal requiring a response from us. The Transcendent apprehended in personal terms as an object of reverence and worship is what we mean by 'God'. Religion so understood is in man a natural impulse, and prayer, whether in word or action, its natural expression.

In my essay entitled *Religion*[1] I have attempted to epitomize and make intelligible the long, strange and often terrible story of man's response to his super-natural environment in the many cults and religions of which history tells. We are too apt to identify religion with Christianity and Christianity with a series of theological doctrines. We have been taught to speak of Christianity as 'the true religion' with the suggestion that all other religions are false. The true religion would be man's right relationship to his super-natural environment, to that reality beyond the world of sense which as an object of worship we call God. All religion is one as man's response to that divine Spirit with which by the necessity of his nature he is inevitably in contact. The Church is not the sole repository of truth. We have now to consider within the sphere of religion what is that distinctive word which Christianity contributes to human thought.

The evolution of this planet, as we understand it, is a continuous process; new forms have ever been appearing, and if their arrival is ultimately inexplicable, we can often

[1] Home University Library.

see how the way for their emergence was prepared. But there have been certain changes or developments so momentous as plainly to mark off a new epoch in the planet's history. One such event, I suppose, would be the moment when the first molecules coalesced and congealed to produce solid objects. The appearance of animate nature is another such event. It may be that there is no absolute distinction between inanimate and animate, no complete breach in nature; borderline cases are perhaps the viruses; but indubitably when what we call 'life' appears, there dawns a new epoch in the planet's history. Another such event is the emergence of mankind. This was not unprepared; we seek and may perhaps have found 'the missing link'; but the coming of man with his reason, his power of forming abstract ideas, his ability to grasp Nature as a whole and to search out its patterns is as inexplicable and epoch-forming as the coming of life itself. What Christians want to say is that in their conviction the coming of Jesus of Nazareth was another such event in the history of the planet. His coming was not unprepared, but human history is rightly divided into the two periods we designate as B.C. and A.D. Some quite new thing has happened which it behoves us all to understand. Because the significance of this event has been traditionally expressed in symbolic or mythological forms which have adequately served previous generations but are misleading and even unintelligible in the twentieth century, we must feel for categories and concepts which will convey and interpret this significance today.

What is this new thing which has happened? Mankind, and more particularly adult and civilized mankind, has long been aware of the Transcendent. This Transcendent has been apprehended as in some sense personal, and religion has been man's personal response to it. But a personal relationship must always be two-sided; I can only know another as that other reveals himself to me, and all apprehension of the Transcendent is by revelation; some kind of initiative in the personal Transcendent which we have called 'God' is presupposed. What Christians apprehend in the coming of Jesus of Nazareth is a quite new revelation of the divine initiative and a new revelation of the nature of the divine.

There is nothing irrational about this view; it would be, so to put it, in line with the story of our planet hitherto. There can be no proving that this has happened, but if Christians can make intelligible to others what it is they see, they may hope that others too will see it.

'God, who commanded the light to shine out of darkness,' wrote the apostle Paul, 'hath shined in our hearts, to give the light of the knowledge of the glory of God in the face of Jesus Christ.'[1] In other words, Christians are declaring an event as new and as wonderful as Creation itself; they have apprehended the glory or presence of God in the person of an historic figure. Something new has occurred upon our planet, like the emergence of life or of man himself. And as each such new emergence is in a sense an explanation of all that has gone before to prepare the way for it, and as there can be no going back upon that which has now occurred, so it is with that happening which may be called the Christ-event.

It remains to explicate this and to make it intelligible so far as may be.

---

[1] II Corinthians iv. 6.

PART II

CHRISTIANITY

IV—THE AMBIGUITIES OF HISTORY

FAITH AND HISTORY

THE Christian faith is irrevocably bound to history. This is its strength, but it raises for thought two serious perplexities. First, there is the haunting dictum of Schelling that necessary truths of reason cannot be deduced from contingent facts of history; second, there is the difficulty of deciding what are 'truths of history' (*Geschichtswahrheiten*).

Against inspissated scepticism it would, I suppose, be impossible to demonstrate beyond imaginable cavil that Alexander the Great or Julius Caesar or Napoleon ever lived. In the case of Jesus, if every alleged fact about him were to be denied or regarded as uncertain, historians would still be compelled to assume that there was some one to account for the rise of the Christian movement, and from this movement they would have to make such inferences as they could about its founder or inspirer. George Santayana once wrote a book in which, drawing from the four Gospels, he presented a homogeneous picture of the Christ-idea; he depicted the Christ of faith in the form of the story of Jesus. This picture was very beautiful but, as he thought, wholly unhistorical. Yet his implicit suggestion that the idea of this unique person, so unlike any of the saints or sages of recorded history, was somehow botched together out of the air by a committee of four who never met is an improbability so extreme as to verge upon the absurd. None the less, to the scientific historian the picture of Jesus presented in the Gospels will appear to be composed of history, legend and symbolism or mythology, and it can never be matter of historical proof that he spoke or acted precisely as is recorded in the Gospels. In recent years leading Protestant scholars such as Bultmann and Tillich have become extremely sceptical of any certainties in the evangelical records. 'Like all historical knowledge, our knowledge of this person (Jesus) is fragmentary and hypothetical,' writes Tillich. 'Historical criticism subjects this knowledge to methodological scepticism and to continuous change in particulars as well as essentials. Its ideal is to reach a high degree of probability, but in many cases this is impossible.' Indeed, while Tillich maintains that 'if the factual element in the Christian event were denied, the foundation of Christianity would be denied', he says that faith cannot even guarantee the name of 'Jesus' in respect of him who was the Christ.[1] All the immense and dedicated labour of scholars upon the Gospels since the rise of scientific methods of historical enquiry, it would seem, has only led to probable results. How can the Christian faith be securely based upon mere probabilities?

Archbishop Whately, if I remember aright, offered a proof that Napoleon was a sun-myth, and I think that a later humorist demonstrated that the author of *In Memoriam* was Queen Victoria; but both these wits agreed that historical scepticism beyond a point is a mark of mental disease rather than of mental acumen. Recognizing that historical research can never attain to more than an extremely high degree of probability I propose first to state the facts about the historical figure of Jesus which, as I suppose, may be regarded as in the highest or in a very high degree probable and may be treated as such by Christians and non-Christians alike; I shall then consider Tillich's observation that the phrase 'the historical Jesus' may properly be used in a quite different sense such as 'raises the question of faith and not the question of his-

[1] *op. cit.* II. 123.

torical research'; faith cannot guarantee the results of historical enquiry, but 'faith does guarantee the factual transformation of reality in that personal life which the New Testament expresses in its picture of Jesus as the Christ'.[1]

THE CONTEMPORARY WITNESS

The proof of the historicity of Jesus does not rest solely upon the New Testament records,[2] nor does it rest primarily on the Gospels, which were written or composed thirty years and more after his death. The only New Testament writer whom scholars will permit us with confidence to call a contemporary of Jesus is the apostle Paul. It is improbable, but possible, that Paul saw Jesus during his earthly life, but certainly he 'knew all about him', as we say. As the leading persecutor of the young Church he accepted the view of those who repudiated Jesus and had caused his death; later he came to know James, the brother of Jesus,[3] Peter and others of the apostolic band; in particular, he made a special journey up to Jerusalem a couple of years after his conversion 'in order to learn Peter's story'.[4] We may therefore rest with confidence upon all that can be safely gleaned from Paul as to the character of Jesus and his teaching.

Professor R. Hawkins has presented a forceful case, based upon alleged logical inconsistencies, for the view that the Pauline letters as we have them have been largely interpolated by a later hand. Even if it be so, the general authenticity of the larger part of the Pauline *corpus* is not in dispute, the alleged interpolations are not connected with the passages I shall cite, and I have made no use of II Thessalonians, Ephesians and, of course, the Pastorals as *antilegomena* or of doubtful origin.

[1] *op. cit.* II. 3.
[2] *v. Das Problem der Geschichtlichkeit Jesu: die ausserchristlichen Zeugnisse*, H. Windisch, *Theologische Rundschau*, 1929, pp. 266 ff.
[3] Galatians i. 19.   [4] Galatians i. 18.

The historicity of Jesus as a human being was regarded by Paul as a matter of first importance;[1] he was born a Jew;[2] he had brothers, James, whom Paul knew personally[3] and others, some of whom were married;[4] his family was believed to be descended from the house of David.[5] As a man and a Jew Jesus worshipped God who is spoken of as his God and Father.[6] As a man Jesus died and was buried.[7] We may add that several hundred persons, some of whom are named, and most of them were alive when the apostle wrote, either saw Jesus or believed that they saw him after his death.[8] We cannot prove any of these facts, but the evidence for them is contemporary and from a responsible person, and there is no reason why they should be questioned.

Of the life of Jesus we learn almost nothing from Paul but of his character much by implication. The Christian character is described by Paul in terms of the Spirit which is the Spirit of God and equally is the Spirit of Jesus.[9] Jesus, he teaches, was the Son of God, and we are sons of God as we are guided by the divine Spirit which is also explicitly the Spirit of Jesus;[10] we are sons because God has sent forth the Spirit of his Son into our hearts.[11] To be guided by the Spirit is to be 'in Christ'; it is to 'put on the Lord Jesus Christ'[12] or, as Moffatt translates it, to 'put on the character of the Lord Jesus Christ'; it is to have Christ 'formed' in us.[13] Paul explicitly states that he 'copies' Jesus;[14] Christians 'have the mind' or share the thoughts of Jesus.[15]

The Spirit or character of Jesus is defined or illustrated in many passages. Paul speaks of 'the pitiful heart of Christ

---

[1] Romans v. 15, 19. I Corinthians xv. 21.
[2] Romans ix. 5. Galatians iv. 4.
[3] Galatians i. 19.   [4] I Corinthians ix. 5.   [5] Romans i. 3.
[6] Colossians i. 3. Romans xv. 6. II Corinthians i. 3., xi. 31.
[7] Colossians i. 22. I Corinthians xv. 3, etc.   [8] I Corinthians xv. 5 ff.
[9] Romans viii. 9.   [10] Romans i. 4, viii. 14. Philippians i. 9.
[11] Galatians iv. 6.   [12] Romans xiii. 14.
[13] Galatians iv. 19. *c.f.* II Corinthians xiii. 5.
[14] I Corinthians xi. i. *c.f.* I Thessalonians i. 6.
[15] I Corinthians ii. 16.

Jesus',[1] of his 'gentleness and reasonableness',[2] of his unquenchable love;[3] he knew no sin, says Paul.[4] Christians are exhorted to shew the humility and helpfulness and forbearance and love of Jesus;[5] Christians are to welcome one another or take one another to their hearts following the example of Jesus;[6] followers of Jesus must exercise a spotless purity in conduct and in word, in integrity of speech and character because the Spirit of Jesus dwells in them.[7]

Jesus is represented as kind and pitying but not as weak. Paul conceived himself to have his authority to deal sharply on occasion;[8] he spoke of the judgement seat, the judgement-day of Christ.[9] But this sternness is that of one who speaks the truth in love, for Christians are to tend their enemies;[10] they are never to return evil for evil; their affections are to know no boundaries, for such is the will of God in Jesus.[11] The coming of Jesus may involve judgement, but it is peace and grace he comes to bring.[12] Joyfulness with patience is explicitly connected with the imitation of Jesus;[13] the kingdom of God is 'righteousness and joy and peace' in the Spirit of Jesus,[14] a Spirit that brings hope and joy and peace and power.[15] In a series of passages Paul sets forth the Christian spirit at some length, as love,[16] as humility, affection, patience, cheerfulness, sympathy, forgivingness,

---

[1] Philippians i. 8.　　　[2] II Corinthians x. i.　　　[3] Romans viii. 35.
[4] II Corinthians v. 21.
[5] Philippians ii. 2–8. *c.f.* Colossians iii. 12–14. Romans xv. 1–3, xii. 14–21.
[6] Romans xv. 7.
[7] Colossians iii. 5–11. Galatians v. 17, 11. Corinthians i. 12, 19. Philippians iv. 8. I Corinthians 15. I Thessalonians iv. 2–10.
[8] II Corinthians xiii. 10.
[9] I Corinthians v. 5. II Corinthians i. 14., v. 10. Romans xiv. 10. Philippians i. 6, 10, ii. 16.
[10] Romans xii. 20.　　　[11] I Thessalonians v. 15 f. 18.
[12] Philippians iv. 17. Colossians iii. 15. I Corinthians 1. 3 f. II Corinthians viii. 9. xiii. 14. Philemon 25.
[13] I Thessalonians i. 6. Romans xii. 12.　　　[14] Romans xiv. 7.
[15] Romans v. 1 f., xv. 13. Colossians iii. 16 f.
[16] I Corinthians xiii. 4–7.

kindly helpfulness,[1] as love, joy, peace, patience, kindliness, integrity, faith, gentleness, self-control,[2] as consideration, self-forgetfulness, gladness and prayerfulness.[3] Such is the quality of him who walks by the Spirit, in whom the character of Jesus is reproduced.

We are here concerned, not with Paul's 'doctrine of the Spirit' nor with his 'Christology', but with the quite plain implications of his letters as to the character of Jesus. Here we see the impression Jesus made on some at least of his contemporaries. This is good historical evidence. It is not reasonable to suggest that this ideal was invented by Paul himself, for indeed he was converted to it; it is as different from the Pharisaic ideal in which he was brought up as it is from the ideal of Aristotle or Confucius.

But all writing of history is inevitably mythistorical; that is to say, if it proceeds, as it must, beyond mere chronicling of facts, it must offer some interpretation and show how the facts may be understood. Even during his lifetime different estimates were made of the significance of Jesus. To some he was the wayward son of the carpenter of Nazareth, to others he was a prophet or even one of the old prophets come back again, some said 'he hath a devil', some wanted to make him 'king' that he might drive the Romans into the sea; Peter on one occasion confessed 'you are the Christ' or 'the Messiah', but how precisely Peter understood that term we cannot say. Mark's Gospel begins with the words, 'this is the beginning of the good news of Jesus the Messiah'; the fourth Gospel was avowedly written 'in order that you may believe that Jesus is the Messiah, the Son of God'. How are we to pass in logic from the reliable 'fact' that Jesus was a person of blameless character to the claims made for him in the New Testament and in all the various theological speculations of the later Christian Church?

[1] Romans xii. [2] Galatians v. 22 f. [3] I Thessalonians v. 12 ff.

We are here in the field, not of logical demonstration but of insight. Many facts are known to scholars and agreed amongst them in respect of our Civil War in the seventeenth century, but no two historians will interpret the agreed facts in precisely the same way. There is nothing 'unscientific' about this inevitable divergence, for in the natural sciences those learned men who have all the facts before them know that these facts must be interpreted, and their interpretation will depend upon their insight. In both science and history out-sight or the knowledge of agreed facts must be interpreted by in-sight or natural genius. There is no means of proving that Jesus of Nazareth is what the Church has claimed that he is, for 'spiritual things are spiritually discerned'. This consideration, however, does not free us from obligation to scientific enquiry and logical consistency.

THE EVIDENCE OF THE GOSPELS

We turn, then, to the secondary traditions of the Gospels. It is proper to ask first how Jesus regarded his own life and task, but here at once we await the inevitable rebuke, 'Sir, thou hast nothing to draw with, and the well is deep.' If it is hazardous to speculate about the self-consciousness of Plato or Cromwell or Napoleon, it is yet more hazardous to speculate about the self-consciousness of Jesus. The well indeed is deep, but we are not entirely without evidence.

The Gospels are documents of faith written a generation after the Master's death; they were put together by men who had no knowledge of what we now regard as the canons of historical enquiry and historical writing. We cannot prove the correctness in detail or the indubitable authenticity of any *pericope* or saying, but there is much in the Gospels that we may accept with reasonable confidence as genuine reminiscence, either because it chimes in with the character of Jesus as we know it from the contemporary evidence, or because there is no reason to suppose that it would have been invented later.

It is, for instance, reasonably certain that Jesus spoke of himself in connection with the 'Son of Man', for this enigmatic phrase, almost meaningless in Greek, would hardly have been repeated again and again in the Gospels apart from some authentic reminiscence. Again, the Hebraic phrase, 'the kingdom of God', as we translate it, must have been used by him in his teaching, for it constantly recurs in the first three Gospels and like the term 'Son of Man' was awkward, needing translation, and was virtually dropped, as the Christian faith was interpreted in the Gentile world. Much the same may be said of the term, 'the Messiah', or 'the Christ', as it is translated into Greek, for very early and within the New Testament itself it becomes virtually a proper name, Jesus Christ or Christ Jesus, and no longer, as it properly is, a title, Jesus who is called the Christ. Scholars have written of 'the Messianic secret', and it is certain that in his lifetime Jesus did not go about proclaiming himself to be the Messiah, for the title had strong political connotations, would have readily been misinterpreted by the crowd and would have attracted the unfavourable attentions of the Roman government. On the other hand, there is no sufficient reason to doubt that Peter at Caesarea Philippi expressed his belief that the Master was 'the Messiah', whatever he understood by the term, that such an event as the so-called Triumphal Entry into Jerusalem was a Messianic act, and that Jesus suffered as 'a false Messiah'.

But if we may be assured that these three terms, 'Son of Man', 'Messiah' and 'kingdom of God' or 'kingdom of Heaven' are closely connected with Jesus' thought about himself or his work, we dare not claim to know with any sort of precision how he understood them. It is, however, of the first importance that all of them, however interpreted by careful scholarship, point to some dramatic, decisive, un-repeatable event in human history or even to the end of human history as known before. There is no kind of reason to doubt that, as we read, Jesus came into Galilee proclaiming that the kingdom of God is at hand, or that he said on another occasion, 'if I by the finger of God cast out demons, without doubt God's kingdom has come upon you', or, rather, words in Aramaic to that effect. The uninstructed modern reader is not excited by these familiar phrases. But to the Jews of that period such a message would involve such a turning over of the heart as today the news that atomic war had broken out. For these Hebraic phrases would convey the message that God was about to intervene or was already intervening in the affairs of men in a way that would involve 'the end of the world' or at least a completely new page in human history. There is no reasonable doubt that this person whose character has by implication been so clearly sketched by the apostle Paul connected his life and work with an event of cosmic significance of this kind.

There are many anecdotes in the Gospels which with every confidence may be accepted as historical reminiscences, such, for instance, as the story of the little Zacchaeus who climbed up a tree to see Jesus, and to whose house, publican though he was, Jesus invited himself to a meal, or the story of the woman who in Simon's house came into the room, broke a valuable box of alabaster and anointed the feet of Jesus, or the story of the woman taken in adultery, though this was no part of the original text of the Gospel; there are very many more. Further, many of the sayings of Jesus recorded in the Gospels and many of the parables, even though we have these words only in a Greek translation, have every mark of authenticity. Nor can there be reasonable doubt that Jesus effected many cures deemed to be 'miraculous', though, of course, no diagnosis of these cases is now available. When Peter is reported to have said as a matter of common knowledge that 'God anointed Jesus of Nazareth with the Holy Spirit and with power, who went about doing good and healing all that were oppressed of the devil, for God was with him',[1] we have interpreted history, but plainly history.

Another not reasonably doubtful element in the Gospel narratives is the indication that Jesus spoke, not as the scribes who were interpreters of documents, but 'with authority'. The prophets of Israel had begun their oracles with the words, 'thus saith the Lord'; Jesus, however, seems to have taught as if he himself had authority to speak in the name of God: 'Moses said . . . but it is I who say unto you',[2] 'it is I that command you, come out of him'.[3] It is the royal voice of authority; it is as the Voice of God. Moreover it seems clear that he connected the coming or present decisive act of God, the bringing in of the kingdom, with his own person and work, and there is good evidence that he connected the new era or the new covenant between God and man with his own death.

A difficult psychological question arises here. I have understated rather than reproduced the claims which Jesus makes for himself implicitly or explicitly in the Gospels. We cannot estimate with any accuracy the degree to which these narratives are coloured by the later theology of the Church, but there seems no reasonable doubt that Jesus as represented here so regarded his person and mission as to give grounds for the observation, 'a sane person, not to say a good person, just could not think of himself in such a way'.[4] Yet the evidence alike for his goodness and his sanity is not to be set aside. We seem to be at a stand. The evidence is self-contradictory. I must offer at least a tentative escape

[1] Acts x. 38.
[2] Matthew v. 22, 28, 34, 39, 44, the pronoun is emphatic in the Greek.
[3] Mark ix. 25.
[4] v. John Knox, *The Death of Christ*, pp. 63 ff, 70.

from the dilemma that we may proceed. 'All that he claims for himself,' wrote Rashdall, 'he claims also for the whole human race through him.'[1] It is, or it may be, of very great significance that the terms 'Messiah', 'Son of Man', 'Son of God' are patient of a corporate and not merely an individual interpretation. The public ministry of Jesus was wholly dedicated to his mission. He was convinced that a moment of crisis had come in human history; he knew what he must do. In the Jewish terminology of the day the terms 'Messiah', 'Son of Man', 'Kingdom of God' stood for the long awaited crisis. That the early Church looking back should have called him personally Messiah, Son of Man, unique Son of God (μονογένης υἱός) was inevitable; that he used these terms of himself in a way to distinguish himself from any who would stand with him is an open question that cannot be decided on dogmatic grounds of faith or unbelief.

I should judge, then, that on the contemporary evidence of the apostle Paul and the second generation evidence of the Gospels there appears a picture about which we might anticipate general agreement among historians whatever their personal prejudices may be. It seems reasonably certain, and there is no good reason why anyone should wish to deny, that in the first century of our era there appeared in Palestine a person of very beautiful character who by his life and teaching created a new ethical ideal clearly distinct from the Judaism from which he sprang or from the ideals of the classical tradition in Europe, in India or in China. For a short time he went about proclaiming 'the kingdom of God', a Jewish phrase pointing to a realized or expected crisis in human history; in connection with this he healed a number of sick people in ways that to his contemporaries appeared miraculous. His message, which could not be separated from his own person, bore, or might be taken to

[1] *Doctrine and Development*, p. 103.

bear, revolutionary political consequences, and because of this he met his death in the peculiarly horrible form then practised by the Roman government on those who were not Roman citizens. 'The Galilean idyll', as it has been called, ended in disaster. We have, however, contemporary evidence that a considerable number of people either saw him, or thought that they had seen him, alive after his death.

There is much here to interest historians, students of manners and moral philosophers. But there is no visible step *per Jesum ad Christum*, from the historical figure to Christology and the speculative faith of Christians. These issues arise in connection with the alleged 'Resurrection' and the indubitable appearance of the early Christian Church. These two subjects are so intimately connected that they cannot be treated in isolation from each other, but they can in theory be distinguished.

RESURRECTION

We are here in a quandary. The Resurrection, if it occurred, was an event in history, but it is not an event with which historians can satisfactorily deal. They cannot reasonably doubt that shortly after his death some hundreds of people saw, or thought they saw, him still alive. Many of these people, as the apostle tells us, were still living when he wrote. But if the historian can be certain that these people saw that which they identified with Jesus, what they really saw is a matter not to be determined by any historical research. The historian can further apply his canons of historical criticism to the legends of the empty tomb and of various appearances of Jesus in Jerusalem, in Galilee, at Emmaus and on the Damascus road. Any competent historian may erect his own theory or interpretation on the basis of these stories, but as an historian he would never claim more than probability for his conclusions, and his view of probability would largely depend not upon his ability as a researcher into history but upon his personal attitude to religion.

The term 'Resurrection' here corresponds to a catastrophic event either in external history or in the minds of the disciples or in both. The Resurrection may have been an external event which could have been photographed had a photographer achieved the anachronism of being present with his camera. But educated Christians are not being intellectually honest if they claim on the basis of their faith to dictate to the historian and to determine *a priori* what must have happened.

Let us suppose for a moment that the holy Sepulchre narratives are substantially accurate, that on Easter Sunday the tomb was empty, that the body of Jesus had not been stolen by his disciples or by anybody else but had 'suffered a sea-change into something new and strange', a transfigured, heavenly body. Let us further suppose that of this the historians have been persuaded. We should then have here an event of unique interest to historians and to scientists of various faculties. But would it be significant for religious thinkers or for religious faith? Of itself it would have much significance, to the great depression of our spirits. This happened, we should say, in this one case; it certainly will not occur in ours. The lowering shadow of unavoidable decay still rests upon all our mortal bodies. If, however, the term 'Resurrection' in the case of Jesus refers to a spiritual event, we may safely leave it to the historians to determine, if they can, whether it also was a physical event.

There can be no doubt that, whatever its physical accompaniments, the 'Resurrection' of Jesus is a name for a spiritual event which can within narrow limits be actually dated and is therefore also an historical event, though as spiritual it be beyond the province of the historian as such. What was this spiritual event?

Historians can record the conversion of St. Paul or of St. Augustine, but it is not as historians but as agnostics or secularists or theologians or psychologists or sociologists that they will attempt to evaluate that which they record. The Resurrection of Jesus can be evaluated in these many ways.

Jesus of Nazareth taught, as we may confidently assert, that God who paints the lilies, feeds the ravens and without whose cognizance not a sparrow falls to earth, cares yet more for human beings who are his children as he is their Father. Let men, therefore, take no thought what they shall eat or what they shall drink or wherewithal they shall be clothed, for their heavenly Father knows that they need these things and can be trusted to provide them; let them, then, without hesitation or qualification dedicate themselves to his cause and put their trust in him. It was a very beautiful picture of an ideal which every man of good will would be eager to believe. The supreme reason for regarding this ideal as a dream, not a reality, is the fate of Jesus himself who taught it. Because of his blameless character and his ardent faith he was the test case of his theory in human history. He died under conditions of savagery and horror, deserted by his friends and, as seemed quite plain, deserted by God himself.

It is reasonable to suppose that his followers suffered a twofold shattering blow. In the first place, they had lost their leader and their friend to whom they owed so much and of whom they hoped so much ('we had hoped that it had been he who should redeem Israel');[1] in the second, their faith in God's providential care of all his children had been shattered. Their faith as well as their friend was gone.

Shortly after his death some of them saw Jesus or thought they saw him. This of itself, though a fact of history, proves nothing. In their distress they might well have been subject to hallucinations. The spiritual and plainly historical fact of

[1] Luke xxiv. 21.

'the Resurrection' is that by some means, through some outward event or inward ecstasy, they became convinced that
after all God had vindicated his Son, that the powers of
religious fanaticism and political expediency had not disposed of him, that he had triumphed over death and over all
that the world could do to him, that he was with them still.
The historian may believe they were mistaken, but that in
fact this conviction came upon them seems quite evident.

The vital question for human beings, whether these early
disciples were deceived in their conviction, is not a matter
that can be settled by historians, logicians or psychologists.
They can see, however, for anyone can see, that as a result
of this inner conviction little societies arose with an *ethos*
or temper and way of life quite different from anything
history had seen before. This *ethos* is reflected in all the
books of the New Testament.

It may be conveniently summed under the one word
'reconciliation', a word which, as Reitzenstein shewed long
ago, really distinguishes Christianity from the mystery cults
that flourished about that time. The Christians believed
themselves to be reconciled to God, their Father, by the
forgiveness of sins; in spite of all sufferings and persecutions
they were reconciled to life as of God's appointment, and
they were reconciled to all their fellow-men in this sense,
that each was a 'brother for whom Christ died'. Church
history is a mottled or ambiguous study; it may be recounted as man's attraction to Jesus of Nazareth and appalling failure to understand him. On the other hand, this sense
of reconciliation with God through the forgiveness of sins,
of reconciliation with life as of God's providential ordering
and of reconciliation with man as embraced by the divine
compassion and in principle our brother may be called the
soul of Church history as it reflects the character and outlook of 'the saints' and in degree of all Christians in so far as
they have been touched by the Spirit of Jesus.

THE DEATH OF JESUS

The appalling death of Jesus was not the disastrous and irrelevant issue of his words and deeds; it is plain from the records that, had he would, it might not dishonourably have been avoided. We may not presume to analyse or discover his thoughts about it. At least during the latter part of his ministry he appears to have tried to tell his disciples that 'the Son of Man' *must* die. There can be little doubt that in some unfathomable way he identified himself with the Suffering Servant in Isaiah,[1] who was numbered with the transgressors, made his grave with the wicked, carried the sorrows and bore the sins of his compatriots; yet God was to vindicate him from the grave, and he was to see of the travail of his soul and thus be satisfied. He was to be a sacrificial victim; in his blood was to be sealed a new covenant between God and man. With some such thoughts in his mind, as it would seem, Jesus went up to Jerusalem to face almost certain death in the incredible confidence that God would vindicate his ultimate fidelity.

Into this Old Testament world it is hard for us, however deep our historical sympathy, to enter. It is, however, very significant, it is perhaps the very fact of the Resurrection, that the Cross of Christ which to all outward appearance was the annihilation of his life, the triumph of his enemies and very negation of that Providence to which he had borne witness, became very soon the symbol of the Christian hope, the Christian Gospel and the Christian victory.

There have been theories about the person of Jesus which have represented him as a supernatural being knowing in advance all that would befall him and almost as acting a stage-part long prearranged. Such a notion is unbiblical and unhistorical. We cannot probe his thoughts, but the evidence points to his conviction that somehow the purposes of

[1] Isaiah liii.

his God and Father in the establishment of his kingdom required his death; therefore, alone and deserted, he faced the unimaginable horrors of his crucifixion in the faith that God would vindicate his action. Human history shows no comparable act of faith in God. The question which no historian as such can answer is whether his faith was justified and his conviction vindicated on the plane of history.

There have been many theories propounded by theologians concerning the death of Christ. With these we are not here concerned.[1] But two non-controversial considerations come home with varying clarity to all Christians everywhere. In his death religious fanaticism and political expediency and the requirements of power-politics and the apathy and ineffectiveness of decent people stand revealed in all their stark defilement. His death was an apocalypse of sin. It was also an apocalypse of love. He could well have avoided death had he loved his people less, but 'having loved his own he loved them unto the end'—and what an end!

In this chapter I have tried to keep to an historical statement which may claim the highest degree of historical probability. In the first century of our era there appeared one in Palestine whose character has brought the world a new ideal; for a few years he went about doing good, healing the sick and giving a teaching which, though we have it but in fragments, in translation and by tradition, has strangely gripped the hearts of men. So far the picture may be called almost universally acceptable. But it seems equally plain that he also taught the imminent arrival of some catastrophic act of God which should turn the course of human history or even bring it to an end; moreover he connected this decisive divine intervention with his own person and work, and it was in the service of this tremendous end that in utter trust in God who should vindicate his faith he

[1] *v. infra*, pp. 128 ff.

refused the way of escape, challenged his enemies in the seat of their power, and went deliberately to his death.

The proof of his vindication or Resurrection, if proof there be, lies not in certain alleged 'appearances' after death, but in the conviction of his disciples and of the infant church and of multitudes ever since, based upon their experience and insight, that all he had taught was true, that he had triumphed over death, and was present with his people who through him were reconciled to God, to life and to their fellow-men.

THE CHRIST-EVENT

So far I have been dealing with historical probabilities. Nothing in history can be proved beyond the possibility of cavil or of question. It is always possible to doubt. In particular, it is very easy, and for most men natural, to doubt whether what I have called the Resurrection as a spiritual event was not an illusion, as the appearances of the living Jesus after his death may be regarded as an illusion. I come back, therefore, to Tillich's use of the phrase 'the historical Jesus' in a form which 'raises the question of faith and not the question of historical research'.[1] The New Testament, he says, 'is an integral part of the event which it documents'.[2] Whatever dubieties may surround the historic figure of Jesus, what we may call 'the Christ-event' is an indubitable fact of history.[3] The 'Christ-event' is the apprehension through certain historical happenings of the divine initiative of grace, the outgoing love of God to sinful men.

Peter Wust's colleague at Münster, his great friend, the professor of mathematics, could never get the philosopher to have any appreciation of the beauty of mathematics;

---

[1] *op. cit.* II. 123.   [2] *op. cit.* II. 134.

[3] Similarly what we may call 'the Buddha-event' is an indubitable fact of history, whatever be the historical uncertainties about Gautama himself.

Peter Wust could not see it; he had no interest here. How frustrated, again, is the musician who tries to explain to the man with no ear for music that a composition by Mozart is not a mere succession of inconsequent and unilluminating notes! Francis Thompson indites an Ode to the Setting Sun:

> High was thine Eastern pomp inaugural;
> But thou dost set in statelier pageantry
>   Lauded with tumults of a firmament:
> Thy visible music-blasts make deaf the sky,
>   Thy cymbals clang to fire the Occident,
> Thou dost thy dying so triumphally:
> I *see* the crimson blaring of thy shawms!

What could he say to one who merely thought the sunset pretty?

This last illustration is happy in that the violent images, even the grotesqueries, of the poet are comparable to some of the imaginative flights of saints and theologians. The 'Christ-event' is not merely that which is recorded in the New Testament; it is still continued. Since the Last Supper of Jesus with the little company in the upper room, every week and perhaps every day his disciples have gathered about the table, broken the bread with thanksgiving and glimpsed 'the glory of God in the face of Jesus Christ'. Of this there is no proof unless it be found in lives transformed by that which they have seen.

Faith is a primary awareness; it is no more susceptible of proof than our awareness of an external world or of the splendour of Beethoven's Fifth Symphony. The Christian faith is based not upon 'contingent facts of history' but upon an awareness of the grace of God which comes to us through history. What are we to say of him who has so brought to us the revelation, the presence and forgiveness of the unseen God?

V—THE SON OF GOD OR 'GOD THE SON'?

THE CHRISTOLOGICAL PROBLEM

THERE is, and there can be, no 'Christological problem' except for those who in some measure have found God through Jesus and his people. Christians are never delivered from the obligations of careful deduction and rigorous logic, but the premises from which they argue here are the spiritual insights or intuitions or experiences which come to them through his life and work. How are we to think of him through whom we are reconciled to God, to life and to our fellow-men?

There are many answers to this question, none of them without value and none of them adequate. The acceptance of traditional formulae by church-going Christians would be a matter of relatively little moment were it not that the use of language not really intelligible or convincing to the mind of our contemporaries is a very serious hindrance to the acceptance of the Christian faith. It is the duty of theologians to translate the Christian intuition into contemporary terms; the traditional formulations will no longer serve.

There have been many attempts, Biblical, Chalcedonian and Reformed, to state or restate the way in which the person of Jesus of Nazareth is to be regarded. It is foolish to ask of any of these traditional formulations 'is it true?' with the underlying assumption that he who does not accept it as 'the truth' is denying the Christian faith. We should ask, rather, is it intelligible, is it comprehensive, is it as adequate as our Christian experience and the limitations of our changing speech allow? Of almost all these traditional formulations we may say that they are true in that they are pointing to the truth, that they are untrue in the sense that they are inadequate or no longer comprehensible by modern men.

In the New Testament Jesus is described in many ways; some poetical, as 'the Dayspring' or 'the bright and morning star'; some theological, as the Messiah, the Lord, the Lamb, the Son of God, the great High Priest; some philosophical as the Second Adam, *the Logos* or the Word of God. For the most part these expressions are metaphorical or pictorial or mythological. That is their weakness and their strength, their strength because poetical or figurative language better than cold prose serves the purposes of liturgy and devotion, their weakness because in the modern world they need much explanation and tend to be partial in their reference.

THE NEW MAN AND THE LOGOS

For our present purposes the two conceptions of Jesus as the Second Adam and as the *Logos* or Word of God are the most significant. Adam is the putative first man. The stories of the Garden of Eden are not to be taken as history. A first man there must have been, but the name Adam means simply 'man' and stands here for humanity before the coming of Christ. But the word 'before' must not here be taken in its usual and purely temporal sense. We divide human history into the two periods 'B.C.' and 'A.D.'; but spiritually most men are still living in the 'B.C.' period. Adam stands for humanity apart from Christ. Paul in the beginnings of his letter to the Romans gives an appalling picture of the moral corruption of the pagan world. But we are not to think of humanity apart from Christ as *massa perditionis*; man was made 'in the image of God'. Those who have lived through the first half of this century do not need to be instructed in the folly, the cruelty, the vice, the bestiality to which human nature, even amongst so-called civilized peoples, is still prone. But apart from Christ modern man is, or is capable of being, rational, gentle, spiritually-minded and religious, capable too, of heroic virtue, but, to use Biblical language, he is 'lost'. This does not mean that he is liable to eternal damnation but simply that he cannot find his way. Modern man is frustrated, he is at cross purposes with himself; he is unreconciled to God, to life and to his fellow-men. He may seek to allay his spiritual dissatisfactions in gross forms or in religious ecstasies, in artistic achievement, in public life or among a select coterie of friends; morally and spiritually he may be far more commendable than many so-called Christians, and even the best of Christians are not delivered from all frustrations, inward tensions and moral failures. But man apart from the Christ is lost, 'moving about in worlds unrealized'. Jesus as the Second Adam is apprehended as the New Man, man in whom human nature at last is fully realized, who looks towards God and upon his fellow-men and upon the experiences that life brings with undistorted vision; he is the Pioneer of a new humanity, and, as in Adam all die, says the apostle,[1] so in Christ shall all be made alive. In some such sense Jesus is called the Second Adam or New Man, the Founder of a new humanity.

In the Old Testament the Word and the Wisdom of God are almost identical in meaning. In the first chapter of Genesis we read that the Word of God inaugurated creation: 'and God said, let there be light, and there was light'; with no difference of meaning the psalmist says, 'the Lord by wisdom founded the earth; by understanding he established the heavens'. The Word of God is, as it were, his Wisdom in action. In later Hebrew literature the Wisdom or Word of God is almost hypostatized or personalized like the Amshaspands in early Mazdaism. So it is

[1] I Corinthians xv. 22.

written of Wisdom in the *Wisdom of Solomon* 'she is a breath of the power of God, and a clear effluence of the glory of the Almighty . . . an effulgence from everlasting light and an unspotted mirror of the working of God and an image of his goodness; and she, though but one, hath power to do all things and, remaining in herself, reneweth all things, and from generation to generation passing into holy souls she maketh them friends of God and prophets.'[1] By the Word or Wisdom of God, then, we understand the expressed mind or purpose or plan of God which inaugurates and supports and informs the universe and which is the inspiration of saints and prophets.

This Word or Wisdom of God, says the author of the Fourth Gospel, was in the beginning; it was with God, indeed it was God:[2] all things were made by the Word, and apart from the Word there was no creation; in the Word was life, and the life was the light of men. If God be conceived in personal terms, this is an intelligible idea. The writer goes on to say that this Word 'became flesh and tabernacled amongst us, and we beheld his glory, a glory as of an only-begotten of the Father, full of grace and truth'.[3] In other words, the writer is saying that Jesus of Nazareth was a human embodiment of the Wisdom or Mind of God.

The apostle Paul says much the same. For instance, he identifies Jesus with 'the Wisdom of God'[4] and declares that in him dwells all the fullness of the Godhead under human conditions or limitations.[5] So, too, the author of the letter to the Hebrews clearly relates the Jesus of history to the Wisdom of God as treated in the Hebrew writings.[6]

[1] VII. 25 ff.

[2] The Word is not here identified with God. When the writer says that the Word was with God, he uses the definite article, ὁ θεός; when he says the Word was God, he says simply θεός, which means more than 'divine' but cannot be translated 'a part of God', for even in man his thought is not a separable part of him.

[3] John i. 1, iv. 14.   [4] I Corinthians i. 24, 30. *c.f.* Colossians i. 15 f.
[5] Colossians ii. 9.   [6] *e.g.* I. 3.

4

We put the wrong question if we ask, 'Is this a doctrine of the divinity of Jesus Christ?'; we are not yet in the realm of doctrine, still less of metaphysics. These writers are saying that in Jesus they have apprehended the very mind and heart and redemptive activity of God under human conditions, or, since the Wisdom or Word of God is in some sense God himself, they are saying that Jesus is in some sense God incarnate, whatever that phrase may mean. In the New Testament we are presented with religious statements or intuitions, not with metaphysical speculations. Here is expressed the central conviction of Christians everywhere. Our theological question is how to put this conviction in terms that will be intelligible and credible to the modern mind.[1]

THE CLASSICAL FORMULATION AND THE 'KENOTIC' SPECULATION

In traditional Christian dogma Jesus is very God and very Man, the God-man, the incarnate second 'Person' of the Trinity. The controversies over the Person of Christ spread across centuries and at last reached a formulation which remains the classical doctrine on this subject. It may be put without misrepresentation, I think, in modern speech like this: human nature is something which all human beings share in common; each of us, John, James, Bartholomew, Philip has his own peculiarity, his own quite distinct centre of consciousness and personality (this distinct individuality corresponds to the old term *hypostasis*); while we all share human nature, the same for all of us, each of us at the centre

[1] It is greatly to be regretted that modern Roman Catholic scholars have gone back upon the identification of Jesus with the Word or Wisdom of God in the Hebrew writings. *v. the Wisdom that is Mary* by C. D. McKonink in *the Thomist*, April, 1943. The writer asks how we may truly 'apply to the Blessed Virgin all that is said of Wisdom in the Sapiential Books'. That the words of Scripture about Wisdom apply to the Virgin Mary he assumes as an accepted doctrine of his Church.

or root of his personality is a created and a fallen spirit; Jesus Christ, according to this doctrine, wholly shared our human nature with us, but the centre or core of his being was not a created and a fallen spirit but the Word or Son of God.

Verbally the Church has strictly maintained the true humanity, as well as the true divinity, of Jesus. The Docetic heresy that his humanity was an appearance only has always been theoretically rejected. But in fact the early discussions were metaphysical arguments not based upon any careful consideration of the Gospel evidence. To this day it may be suspected that for most Christians Jesus is an unreal figure, a heavenly visitor, a pre-existent being who for a few years lived a human life, one who was temporally a human being in appearance but is metaphysically a part of Godhead. Indeed the classical doctrine of his Person explicitly denies that he was a man at all: he became Man, he did not become *a* man; he wore human nature as a garment, but he was always the eternal Word or Son of God, and was not *a* man.

Such a picture of him, however true it may be to the Christian feeling about Jesus, must be rejected as unhistorical. The crucial issue is the prayers of Jesus; there is no doubt that he prayed; we read, and have no reason (except our own theories) to doubt, that he spent whole nights in prayer. God according to the New Testament is 'the God and Father of our Lord Jesus Christ',[1] the God and not the Father only. Jesus was a man, the man of Nazareth. This does not imply that the spiritual intuition upon which the classical doctrines rest must be treated as an error, but we are quite untrue to our historical conscience if we erect any theory which makes nonsense of the evidence that he was a real man, that he walked by faith and lived in the strength of prayer.

The other main traditional approach to the doctrine of

[1] Romans xv. 6. II Corinthians xi. 31. Ephesians i. 3. I Pet. i. 3.

the Person of Christ has been based on Philippians ii. 6—11 and is hence called the Kenotic. It is argued that God, while not ceasing to be God and to rule the universe, in some way 'emptied himself' of some of his attributes and came to earth in human guise. This, frankly, is pure mythology. When Charles Wesley wrote:

> He left His Father's throne above—
> So free, so infinite His grace—
> Emptied Himself of all but love,
> And bled for Adam's helpless race.
> 'Tis mercy all, immense and free;
> For, O my God, it found out me!

we can accept this as poetry, as an expression of the profound vision and religious experience of the poet; many Christians will find in it a statement far more satisfactory to heart and mind than the prosaic discussions of the theologians, but poetry and mythology are not technical theology.

Perhaps the sense of awe, of wonder, of mystery, of ecstasy with which the deeply experienced Christian contemplates the Cross of Christ has never been better expressed than in another stanza by Charles Wesley:

> O Love divine! what hast Thou done?
> The immortal God hath died for me!
> The Father's co-eternal Son
> Bore all my sins upon the tree;
> The immortal God for me hath died!
> My Lord, my Love is crucified.

Even to many Christians such language may seem extravagant and intellectually confusing; it is open to unanswerable criticism if taken in any sort of literal sense; it may even be thought unwise to use language which is liable to such devastating misinterpretation. But the stanza is no more 'untrue' (or, if it be preferred, is no more 'true') than Titian's *Assumption of the Virgin Mary* or Milton's *Ode on the Nativity*. What is required of theologians, however, is some intelligible statement about Jesus of Nazareth which will be adequate to explain the music, the poetry, the paintings, the mythologies which have arisen out of the awareness of God which has come to Christian men through him.

We have clearly come to a point where, as in old-fashioned novels, the writer may directly address the reader. The reader of novels was always the 'gentle' reader. The reader of theology is apt to be the infuriated reader. I am well aware from long experience that what I am now saying is certain to be misread and misunderstood by many a faithful Christian unless he will make a firm and deliberate effort not to assume that I am saying what in fact I am not saying. I am not saying it is untrue that Jesus is the Son of God, or that he ascended into the heavens and sitteth at the right hand of God, or that he is both God and man. What I am saying is that these and many similar expressions, however metaphorically or symbolically or spiritually true, and however devotionally satisfying, are not *literally* true; God can only metaphorically or analogically be said to have a Son; God has no right hand, nor could his dwelling-place be located in the sky above the soil of Palestine; the uncreated God cannot become created, for, as Tillich says, 'the assertion that "God has become man" is not a paradoxical but a nonsensical statement'.[1] Much of the traditional phraseology of Bible and theology, of hymn and liturgy, may be natural or even inevitable upon the lips of faith. But the modern world looks to the Church for intellectual integrity, and often thinks it looks in vain. We are not called to say that the traditional, metaphorical, mythological, poetical language is 'untrue'; the Christian Gospel remains what it always was, but we are under the most urgent obligation, if the modern world is to become Christian, to speak of him in terms that will seem real and intelligible in the language and thought-forms of today. Two principles, in particular,

[1] *op. cit.* II., p. 109.

we must uphold, the unity of the Godhead and the real humanity of Jesus; both of these are jeopardized in popular and often in professional theology.

THE TRINITARIAN FORMULA

Since Jesus is often spoken of as 'the Second person of the Trinity' or 'God the Son', it seems necessary at this point to animadvert upon the traditional Trinitarian doctrine of the Godhead.

The Church has always asserted in theory the unity of God, as it has asserted in theory the true humanity of Jesus, but the doctrine of the Trinity, as usually expounded, cannot be said to safeguard either of these principles. Leonard Hodgson, for instance, can speak of three centres of consciousness in the Godhead, and liturgiologists can address prayers to the different 'Persons' of the Trinity. Indeed, even the most 'orthodox' theologians find the greatest difficulty in expounding their doctrine without giving the impression, and at times actually implying, that God is three personalities who yet mysteriously are somehow one. Moreover, it is not unfairly claimed by Farnell that popular Christianity has not been truly monotheistic in so far as it has contrasted the divine man, attractive and appealing, with the supreme, remote, Judaic God.[1] The consequent inconveniences are very great: the ordinary church-going Christian, who cannot possibly understand the complicated metaphysical doctrine which the theologians expound, accepts 'the doctrine of the Trinity' as a mystery beyond his comprehension; the theologians of what is now regarded as

---

[1] *The Attributes of God*, p. 93. Farnell also says that 'Judaism and Islam are the only world-religions that have been able to keep out the goddess; and therefore they are the only religions that have been able to maintain themselves as pure monotheisms', p. 48. Theologically this is an unfair comment, for Christianity has never recognized the Virgin Mary as a goddess; but it raises an important point to which I shall come shortly.

'orthodoxy' are maintaining a doctrine which can hardly be stated without contradictions and lapses into 'heresy',[1] and a quite needless stumbling-block is placed in the way of the understanding of the Christian faith by the non-Christian world. The Christian doctrine of the Godhead must not be unintelligible to all except professionals.

In Trinitarianism the number three is quite secondary, as Tillich says.[2] If the early theologians had written of Christ as the incarnation of the divine Spirit and had thus not distinguished between 'the Son' and 'the Spirit', their theology might have developed upon different lines without implying any difference in their religious apprehension; or if they had thought fit to say that God is manifested first as the Ground of being, second as the divine Wisdom 'sweetly ordering all things in heaven and earth', third, in the incarnate Word, and fourth, as the holy Spirit known in the communion of the Church, their apprehension of God would have been in no way different from that expressed in the trinitarian formula.

I am not asserting that the doctrine of the Trinity is 'untrue', and, indeed, I will indicate that from some aspects a trinitarian formula is inevitable; but this inevitability might not have been seen, and the number three is not important or significant. The Christian faith can, indeed, be summed up in the Trinitarian formula, but where this formula is not made intelligible and inevitable, it serves as a

---

[1] The source of the confusion is fourfold: first: because 'the Word' of God, itself an analogy, is said to be 'generated' by 'the Father', 'the Word' is called 'the Son'; then the term 'God the Son' is identified with 'the Son of God', which is a name applied in the New Testament to Jesus in a religious, not a metaphysical sense; second, 'the Son' in this doctrine has to be clearly distinguished from 'the Spirit', which in the New Testament is identified with the Spirit of Jesus or Jesus present in the Spirit; third, there is no English word corresponding to the meaning of *persona* in the original doctrine, and the three 'Persons' of the Trinity tend inevitably to be regarded as in some sense persons; fourth, there is no intelligible relation between the *assumptus homo* and 'God the Son'.

[2] *op. cit.* I., p. 252.

hindrance to the understanding and acceptance of the Christian faith. It is not a divinely revealed 'mystery' but a doctrine worked out in various ways after centuries of Christian speculation.

There is no one single Christian doctrine of the Trinity, for there are many.[1] The colour or content or religious significance of the doctrine is always derived from the Christian apprehension of the divine self-revelation in the person of Jesus, and therefore it seems improper in theology as in logic to treat this doctrine apart from a discussion of Jesus himself. 'The doctrine of the Trinity,' writes Tillich, 'can be discussed only after the christological dogma has been elaborated.'[2] None the less, the doctrine of the Trinity is a doctrine of the Being of God, not a doctrine about Jesus. There are what Tillich calls 'trinitarian principles', and, as he says, 'the trinitarian principles appear whenever one speaks meaningfully of the living God'.[3] As I hope to shew, the doctrine of the Trinity is in almost all its forms a mode of stating that God is to be personally conceived; the distinctively Christian element in the doctrine is that, in view of that which we apprehend through 'the divine missionary of the New Testament',[4] it is as personal Love that God is to be conceived.

But in saying that the doctrine of the Trinity is a doctrine of the Being of God, not a doctrine about Jesus, I seem to run counter not merely to tradition but also to so free and modern a scholar as Professor Farmer. Central to Christian worship, he says, is the faith 'that Jesus is God incarnate'.[5] Later he says, 'the doctrine of the Trinity, summed up in the triune name, affirms that the Father-Son relationship which characterized the historic consciousness of Christ as set before us in the Gospels is constitutive of the very

---

[1] v. R. S. Franks, *The Doctrine of the Trinity*, in the Duckworth series.
[2] *op. cit.* I. 279.   [3] *ib.*   [4] Walter Pater.   [5] *op. cit.*, p. 48.

essence of God'.[1] I cannot pass by so weighty a denial of that which I have written in the preceding paragraph without comment, nor is my comment complete till we have carried the discussion further.

First, I would observe that the traditional doctrine of Christendom has been that Jesus is 'the Word' or 'the Son' of God incarnate; he is not the Trinity incarnate, and therefore the bare statement that 'Jesus is God incarnate' is open to misunderstanding and, I suspect, is technically 'heretical'. Second, Dr. Farmer sets Jesus 'in his filial relation to the Father within the Godhead',[2] but it is one thing to say that the filial consciousness of Jesus or the Father-Son relationship between God and Jesus is essential to, and determinative of, the Christian understanding of God, but to say that a relationship of 'the man Christ Jesus' to his God and Father is itself 'within the Godhead' or is 'constitutive of the very essence of God' raises such intolerable difficulties for thought that we must at least hope that in the sequel some happier phraseology may be suggested.

'God in three Persons, blessed Trinity' is a phrase familiar in traditional Christian worship. What does the word 'Person' mean in this context? The term *persona* which it translates, does not mean an individual person or a personality; it is a technical theological term which, when it is used in public, is today bound to be misleading or misunderstood. Peter Lombard and St. Thomas Aquinas, following St. Augustine, assert that 'the love by which we love God and our neighbour is the Holy Spirit'; St. Augustine had said, 'the Holy Spirit is the love wherewith the Father loves the Son and the Son the Father'.[3] In St. Thomas *proprietas* is a synonym for *persona*; by the three *proprietates*, says Rashdall, 'we may, perhaps, understand

---

[1] *op. cit.*, p. 58.   [2] *ib.*, p. 58.
[3] Peter Lombard, *Sententiae*. I. 1. dist. xvii; St. Thomas, *Summa Theol.* I.Q. xxxvii. St. Augustine, *de Trinitate*. vi. 5. *c.f.* Rashdall, *Doctrine and Development*, pp. 21 ff.

three distinct and essential properties or powers or activities or modes of existence'. 'Permanent mode of being' is Raven's translation of *persona*;[1] 'way of being' is Karl Barth's.[2] Abelard illustrates three modes of existence in one essence by a signet ring: it is gold, it is an engraving, it is that which seals.[3]

What, then, are the modes of being intended when it is said that God exists 'in three Persons'? Very varied answers are given, though the answers are always related to the traditional formula, Father, Word (or Son) and holy Spirit. St. Augustine found in the human mind the best analogy to the Being of God as man can conceive him; there is the knower corresponding to the Father, that which it knows corresponding to the Word (or Son), and there is the feeling of the knower for that which he knows corresponding to the Spirit. If a man expresses his love for his wife, we can distinguish in logic (but only in *logic*) between the thinker, his thought (the idea of his wife) and the love with which he entertains his thought. It is only by a process of logical abstractions that we can make these distinctions, for the thinker does not exist apart from his thought, nor does his thought exist without his love. If we think of God as personal, we are bound to imagine him as including Thinker, his Thought (or Word) and the relation between Thinker and Thought (or Word). In theological terms this has been expressed as the Father, the Word and the Spirit, or, since the thinker generates his thought, we may speak of the Father, the Son and the Spirit. This is the sense in which St. Augustine says that the holy Spirit is the love wherewith the Father loves the Son and the Son loves the Father.

Again (I quote from Rashdall), 'God is Power and God is Wisdom and God is Will—that is the recognized scholas-

---

[1] *Experience and Interpretation*, p. 147.
[2] *Dogmatics in Outline*, p. 42.
[3] *Epitome Theologiae Christianae*, III. 12.

tic explanation of the doctrine of the Holy Trinity. Or, since the Will of God is always a loving Will, the School-men tell us that the Holy Spirit may indifferently be spoken of as Will or as Love; from the union of Power and Wisdom in God's nature there proceeds a loving Will'.[1] As the signet ring is a three in one, says Abelard, so is God *omnipotens, omnisapiens, omnibenignus.*[2] St. Bonaventure on Mount Alvernia contemplated the Blessed Trinity as Love, Truth, Holiness.[3] Elsewhere, in one of his great hymns, Abelard speaks of God 'from whom, through whom and in whom are all things; him from whom are all things we call the Father, through whom are all things the Son, and in whom are all things the Spirit'.[4] Not dissimilarly Karl Barth in our own day speaks of 'God the Creator, God in his action in Jesus and in his operation as the holy Spirit'.[5] The doctrine of the Trinity is a doctrine about God, not about Jesus.

The term 'Son' came to be preferred to the term 'Word' because of the unique relationship recognized by Christians between Jesus of Nazareth and God, but this is the christo-logical issue with which we are not now concerned. In the doctrine of the Trinity as traditionally held in the Christian Church 'Son' and 'Word' are interchangeable terms. 'Word' is used because the Thought of God is conceived as being not merely his thought within himself but also as his uttered thought. So St. Thomas quotes from Psalm xxxiii. 9, *dixit et facta sunt,*[6] 'for it was he who spoke—and earth existed'.[7] He is quite explicit that the Word of God covers all creation, 'for God in knowing himself knows every creature'; the

---

[1] *Doctrine and Development*, p. 26.   [2] *ibid.*
[3] Gilson, *the Philosophy of St. Bonaventure*, p. 78.
[4] *Perenni Domino perpes sit gloria,*
  Ex quo sunt, per quem sunt, in quo sunt omnia.
  Ex quo sunt Pater est, per quem sunt Filius,
  In quo sunt Patris et Filii Spiritus.
[5] *Dogmatics in Outline*, p. 42.   [6] Psalm xxxii. 9 in the Vulgate.
[7] Moffatt's translation.

Word, writes Gilson in exposition of St. Bonaventure, 'necessarily contains the archetypes of all the possible imitations of God, whatever their degree of perfection may be'.[1] It is difficult to be more 'orthodox' than St. Thomas. The term 'the Son' therefore covers all creation.

It is of much importance that in the classical doctrine of the Trinity, as Moberly admits, the name 'Son' is only used analogically of the pre-existent Word.[2] God is to be personally conceived and, as we learn pre-eminently if not solely through Christ, he is personal Love. This is the doctrine of the Trinity as the Christian doctrine of the Being of God.

Some later doctrines of the Trinity are statements not so much of the Being of God as of his self-revelation. Schleiermacher, for instance, held that the transcendent God is known in the Universe, in Christ and in the Church; thus is he revealed as Father, Son and Holy Spirit. So Dr. Karl Barth, at least sometimes, takes the Trinity to be a Trinity of revelation, as he identifies Father, Son and Holy Spirit with the subject, the form and the contingency of revelation, though no doubt, that which we learn in revelation must be carried back into the eternal Being of God.[3]

Trinitarian principles, says Tillich on the other hand, are 'moments within the process of the divine life';[4] they represent a qualitative, not a numerical, characterization of Deity. 'Human intuition of the divine,' he writes, 'always has distinguished between the abyss of the divine (the element of power) and the fullness of its content (the element of mean-

---

[1] *Deus enim cognoscendo se, cognoscit omnem creaturam. Verbum igitur in mente conceptum est repraesentativum omnis eius quod actu intelligitur. Unde in nobis sunt diversa verba secundum diversa quae intelligimus. Sed quia Deus uno actu et se et omnia intelligit, unicum verbum eius est expressivum non solum Patris sed etiam creaturarum, St. Thomas Summa Theologica, Pars Prima. quaest. xxxiv. art. 3.* Gilson, *op. cit.*, p. 143, *c.f.* pp. 146 f.

[2] *Atonement and Personality*, ch. viii. v. Franks, *The Doctrine of the Trinity*, p. 185.

[3] *v.* Franks, *op. cit.*, pp. 180, 184, 198.   [4] *op. cit.* I., p. 277.

ing), between the divine depth and the divine *logos*. The first principle is the basis of Godhead, that which makes God God. It is the root of his majesty, the unapproachable intensity of his being, the inexhaustible ground of being in which everything has its origin.'[1] The term *Logos* or Word 'unites meaningful structure with creativity'. The Spirit is the actualization of these two principles; 'both power and meaning are contained in it and united in it. It makes them creative'.

The doctrine of the Trinity asserts that within the Godhead there are three modes of existence, the Father, the Word (or Son) and the Spirit. The term 'Father' is used instead of some neutral term such as the Ground of all being because it is desired to assert that the Ground of all being is personal, and because Christians have learnt through Jesus, and indeed from the Old Testament also, to address as Father that incomprehensible Being who is the Ground of all existence; 'God hath sent forth the Spirit of his Son into your hearts crying Abba, Father'.[2] But the Ground of all being is not to be conceived as of the masculine gender. God is not more like a man than like a woman. We read perhaps in Scripture that of the divine Fatherhood all human fatherhood is named,[3] but it might as truly and properly be said that of the divine Motherhood all motherhood in heaven and earth is named. This is a matter of no small importance. I cited earlier Farnell's view that Christianity has not succeeded in keeping out the goddess,[4] and Protestants have always protested with full justification that the cult of the Virgin Mother of God in Roman and Orthodox churches has no justification in Scripture and is in practice, though never in theory, a reintroduction of the goddess into religion; but the cult represents a true religious insight. In one of the early Eastern pseudepigrapha the

---

[1] *op. cit.* I, pp. 277 f.   [2] Galatians iv. 6.
[3] Ephesians iii. 14. R.V. *margin.*   [4] *v. supra,* p. 102.

clause occurs, 'the holy Ghost is my Mother'. That was possible because in the Semitic languages the word for Spirit is feminine as it is not in Greek and Latin. By 'God the Father' we mean the Ground of all being whose relationship to us we conceive to be that of which human parentage is some faint reflection.

For the avoidance of grave theological confusion and intellectual scandal it is important clearly to distinguish the two terms 'Son of God' and 'God the Son'. The former is a religious term, the latter a theological. Jesus is called 'the Son of God' and, indeed, 'the unique Son of God'[1] because of his unbroken filial relationship with his heavenly Father. 'God the Son' is identical in meaning with 'the Word' which, as St. Thomas makes clear, covers all creation. It is therefore quite improper to identify Jesus with 'God the Son', but on the other hand it is entirely meaningful (and incidentally solely 'orthodox') to say that in Jesus we see the Mind, the Thought, the Character, the Purpose of God incarnate so far as this is possible under human limitations or σωματικῶς, as the apostle puts it.

The term 'Spirit' is much more difficult to define but, curiously, is much less in need of definition. When we speak of 'high spirits' or 'a spirit of gentleness' or say of someone that he may be very clever but we do not like his spirit, our meaning is not obscure. Similarly we can speak intelligibly about a divine Spirit with which we feel our own spirits, at least on occasion, to be in contact. If we were to say that in Jesus we see the divine Spirit incarnate in a human being, we should, indeed, deviate from 'orthodox' phraseology, but there would be no distinction in meaning from the assertion that he is the Word of God incarnate.

I am not interested to defend the traditional trinitarian formula; a better formula, it may be, could be found. What is vital in the formula is this: God, the Ground of all being,

[1] μονογένης υἱός.

is to be personally conceived; moreover, he does not exist in lonely *perseitas*, existing, that is, in solitary enjoyment of his own being; his Word or Thought is uttered; it creates the world; his divine Spirit suffuses all creation; he is not merely the Absolute of the philosophers, the Transcendent, the Wholly Other; he is the living and redeeming God of Love.

Oman observes that 'learned terminology has always assumed the right to confer impressiveness';[1] moreover, many learned scholars would agree that the mystery of the Godhead has never been more admirably stated than in the so-called 'Athanasian Creed'. But St. John Chrysostom has a saying πάντα τὰ ἀναγκαῖα δῆλα, 'all things needful are plain'. God is personal Love embracing his creation; that is the meaning or substance of the 'Athanasian Creed'. If this were made plain to the ordinary Christian and to the world outside, the understanding and presentation of Christianity would be much simpler.

[1] *op. cit.*, p. 275.

VI—GRACE INCARNATE

Du den wir suchen auf so finsteren Wegen,
Mit forschenden Gedanken nicht erfassen,
Du hast dein heilig Dunkel einst erlassen
Und tratest sichtbar deinem Volk entgegen.

TOWARDS A MODERN CHRISTOLOGY

(a) *Karl Barth.* Karl Barth is the theologian of the Word of God. This Word is that which is preached in the living Church, that to which the prophets and apostles testify in the pages of Scripture, that which is incarnate in Jesus of Nazareth and that which is heard in the believer's heart. Of this living and vivifying Word, he says, there is no doubt; the historians may do their best or their worst, but no evidence of theirs can qualify the Word or render it ineffectual. In his very courageous book, *The Humanity of God*, comparable to the *Retractationes* of St. Augustine, Barth repudiates the idea of God as the Wholly Other in a sense which makes any divine self-communication unintelligible. Christ, he says, is the Revealer alike of God and of man. Barth rejoices in the phrase 'the humanity of God' (*laetum et ingens paradoxon*, as Bengel would say); it belongs to the sovereign freedom of God, which is a freedom to love and therein to give himself to man.[1]

But Barth for all his vast learning, his remarkable insights and his very sufficient prolixity, while he magnificently declares the Christian faith, is of very little help to us in our immediate quest, for he uses, and even revels in, the traditional language of the Church. There are three modes of

[1] *op. cit.*, pp. 47–49.

existence in God, he tells us; of these one mode is the Word which is the Son. Since he follows the traditional language, Barth can hardly avoid speaking of the Son as a separate agent from the Father and the Spirit and even as a separate consciousness.[1] He rejects any christology 'which aims at making the human nature, the historical and psychological manifestations of Jesus as such, its object'.[2] For the incarnation 'comes to us as datum with no point of contact with any previous datum'.[3] Barth's 'starting point' is 'the fact that the eternal Word of God chose, sanctified and assumed human nature and existence into oneness with himself, in order thus, as very God and very Man, to become the Word of reconciliation spoken by God to man'.[4] The incarnation is not one of creation's evolutionary possibilities; it is a mystery; 'the incarnation of the Logos is not a change from his own nature or his own mode of being as the divine Word into the nature and mode of being as a creature, nor yet the rise of a third thing between God and man'; 'he was made flesh in the entire fullness of deity, which is also that of the Father and of the holy Spirit'.[5] The manhood of Jesus is only the predicate of the Word, who is the Lord, acting upon us; it is not improper to use the term *Theotokos* or Mother of God for the Virgin Mary; 'the incarnation is inconceivable, but it is not absurd, and it must not be explained as an absurdity'.[6]

But while Barth asserts the incarnation as the *unio hypostatica*,[7] and is unhelpful for our present purposes because he uses the language of tradition which is only intelligible to scholars, he insists more emphatically and more daringly than almost any other theologian upon the true humanity of Jesus, in whom the Word became 'a real man'; in becoming Jesus the Word 'did not cease to be what

---

[1] v. *Church Dogmatics*, I. 2, pp. 160 f.   [2] ib., p. 136.
[3] ib., p. 172.   [4] ib., pp. 122, 124.   [5] ib., pp. 131, 133 f., 136.
[6] ib., pp. 138, 160, 162.   [7] ib., p. 165.

he was before, but he became what he was not before, a man, this man'; he assumed our fallen human nature; he was not 'an ideal man'; for us he was made sin.[1] Can we understand this or translate it into modern intelligible terms?

(b) *John Oman*. 'The divinity of Jesus, set forth by itself as a metaphysical principle and apart from the humanity it inspired and sustained and the love of the Father which appeals through it, reduces the humanity to an illusion and the divinity to an abstract symbol,' says Oman.[2] He holds that while Jesus was 'on the physical side' born in a Jewish family, on the spiritual side he was God's Son 'by a spirit of holiness, and was exalted by way of loyalty, most conspicuously manifested on the Cross'; he was sinless, not because he was a divine being beyond the reach of temptation but because his communion with the Father was unbroken. Oman justifies or vindicates the apostle Paul's language about Jesus, whom he calls the Son, the likeness, the fullness of God, the heavenly man, the heavenly Christ, the Second Adam, by reference to the obscure statement in Genesis that man is made in God's image and by reference to Philo's interpretation of this as meaning that the ideal man is the Image, Son or Word of God. Jesus, the ideal man, is, then, the Son of God, not in virtue of any metaphysical difference from us in his nature but as the perfect human reflection of God;[3] he is what we ought to be through him. At first sight this may appear a very humanistic and rationalistic and unevangelical point of view, but we should remember that Jesus is the Image of God in his outgoing love and reconciling grace to outcasts, to sinners, to the undeserving. This view is therefore fully consonant with the apostle's declaration that God was in Christ reconciling

---

[1] pp. 147, 149, 151, 153, 157.   [2] *Honest Religion*, p. 96.
[3] *Honest Religion*, pp. 104 f.

the world to himself. I should interpret Oman's hints in some such way as this: all men are made in the image of God; it is only as God is in us or, better, as we are in God that we exist at all; Jesus did not differ from us here; where he differed is that his life was wholly suffused with the divine life like a red-hot rod of iron in which metal and fire are inseparable from each other, and which manifests therefore the nature of fire through the nature of the metal. Such was the historical Jesus as apprehended by faith but not as demonstrable by historians.

(c) *Hastings Rashdall.* Rashdall similarly protests against 'a metaphysical Christ, whose humanity was, indeed, acknowledged in word, but who lacked all the attributes of the humanity which we know'.[1] He recognizes the mystery of the person of Jesus in that one such as he cannot be 'the mere chance product of evolutionary forces';[2] it is therefore natural or even necessary to use of him such mythological language as that God sent his Son. God is ever communicating himself to man—through beauty, through the demands of love and loyalty, through his saints, his prophets and his heroes—but in Jesus we apprehend 'a supreme act of God's self-communication to the world'[3] in the manifestation of a love that extends to the unthankful, the unworthy, the outcasts, the publicans and sinners, and which on the Cross was manifest as love and forgiveness beyond measure.

(d) *William Morgan.* One of the most fearless and rigorous of thinkers in recent years was my one-time colleague and friend, William Morgan, of Queen's University in Canada. He may be taken as the representative of the Ritschlian tradition. He maintains that, except when merely traditional language has been repeated, the Church's thought of Christ has always been expressed in the current philosophical or

---

[1] *Doctrine and Development*, p. 94.   [2] *ib.*, p. 106.   [3] *ib.*

quasi-philosophical language of the age. As a modern man and a Ritschlian, therefore, he attempts to express the significance of Jesus in terms of value-judgements. 'Jesus,' he says, 'is the supreme Pioneer in the field of religious knowledge. In the unerring clearness of his moral judgements and the intensity of his feeling for moral reality he stands in history unapproached and unapproachable. He is the incarnate conscience of mankind . . . The second element in Jesus' significance is his faith in God . . . The faith of Jesus in itself and apart from what was new in its content was a reality potent enough to mark an epoch in religion . . . Again, in a degree which is altogether unique, Jesus is one with the kingdom of righteousness, truth and love which he proclaimed . . . Jesus is the leader of mankind in the highest things, the one figure in all history whom we can follow without reserve . . . Finally, Jesus, as none other, embodies in his life those great moral realities in which God reveals himself to us and lays his hand upon us . . . Summing up, we can say that in Jesus we find a religion we can believe, a leader we can follow—one whose faith supports ours—and the presence and working of the living God as the God of our salvation . . . Jesus is not only touched with the Divine, as many are; he is all Divine. The Divine constitutes the whole content of his human life.'[1] It is not possible to shew, says Morgan, that 'Jesus appears in history as a visitor from the transcendent world. Our belief in his unique significance is the product, not of any theoretical proof that he does not belong to the world of time and change, but of our feeling for the eternal values embodied and expressed in his personality and teaching'.[2] This is very different from the language of Chalcedonian theology, very different from the warm and passionate language of traditional evangelical preaching. But we have here language that the modern man

---

[1] *The Nature and Right of Religion*, pp. 106–110.
[2] *op. cit.*, pp. 290 f.

can understand, and we should carefully consider whether all the insights of historical theology and Christian devotion cannot be expressed within this framework.

(e) *Donald Baillie*. Somewhere in his *Journal* John Wesley records that coming downstairs one morning he met a tittering servant-girl. He looked at her, said to her 'be serious' and passed on. Returning years later he learnt that these two unrehearsed and almost casual words had gone home to the girl's heart and had been the first stimulus of her conversion. Well might John Wesley have reflected, as no doubt he did, 'not I but the grace of God through me'. Many Christians must be aware that at some time or another they, consciously or unconsciously, have been instruments of the grace of God; it is very mysterious, and, when they learn of it, they are humbled and thankful. We have probably known a few people, saints we call them, who are constantly ministering the Word of God to those about them, making God's presence real to them, as we say, making real to them the grace or the will or the forgiveness of their heavenly Father. Donald Baillie led us to think of Jesus as one who so constantly lived in the presence of God that the words he spoke were always the words of God to his hearers, and the deeds he did always the acts of God.[1] 'The Son doeth nothing but what he *seeth* the Father do'; the Son sayeth nothing but what he *heareth* the Father say. Such an intimacy between Jesus and his heavenly Father goes out immeasurably beyond anything we know by experience, but it is intelligible to us. If we can sometimes say 'not I but the grace of God in me', he, it would seem, could always say, 'not I but the grace of God in me'. That would be not a christological theory but an attempt to state the facts about Jesus. If those be the facts, it would be very natural to say, using metaphorical or symbolical language, that he was

[1] *God was in Christ.*

the incarnation of the grace of God, or was God manifest in human life.

(f) *Paul Tillich*. No man has wrestled more painfully, as the Puritans would say, with the attempt to find intelligible terms in which to express the person of Jesus as Christians apprehend him than has Paul Tillich. Jesus walked in perfect communion with the God of our salvation; he 'is completely transparent to the mystery he reveals'.[1] Tillich points to 'his victory over every temptation to exploit his unity with God as a means of advantage to himself', hence 'he who believes in me, does not believe in *me*'.[2] In all his utterances, deeds and sufferings Jesus is 'transparent to that which he represents as the Christ, the divine mystery' of God's initiative in our salvation.[3] As St. Ambrose put it, we behold

> *in Patre totus Filius*
> *et totus in Verbo Pater.*

Thus Jesus is 'the miracle of the final revelation, and his reception is the ecstasy of the final revelation'.[4] Not Christianity, but that to which it witnesses, is final.[5] In Jesus as the Christ we apprehend a concrete absolute; here, as in the phrase the God-man, we are in the presence of that which is logical paradox and even contradiction, for, as Tillich says, the perfectly concrete and the perfectly absolute cannot be expressed in terms of the structure of reason but only in terms of the depth of reason.[6] The old 'Two Natures' doctrine of Christ's person will no longer serve us; we cannot comprehend the divine nature, and if we speak of human nature, we certainly do not mean by it that which was intended by the authors of that doctrine.[7] What we can say is that 'in Jesus as the Christ the eternal unity of God

---

[1] *op. cit.* I., p. 148.   [2] John xii. 44. Tillich, *op. cit.* I. 151.
[3] *ib.*   [4] *op. cit.* I., p. 152.   [5] *op. cit.* I., p. 150.
[6] *op. cit.* I., pp. 166 f.   [7] *v.* Tillich, *op. cit.* II., p. 167.

and man has become historical reality'.[1] 'The conquest of existential estrangement in the New Being, which is the being of the Christ, does not remove finitude and anxiety, ambiguity and tragedy; but it does have the character of taking the negativities of existence into unbroken unity with God'.[2]

Tillich always writes from the background of the agonies through which in his lifetime the world has been passing, and his vocabulary is difficult, but it is plain that he is trying to express the same insight as that of earlier generations who spoke of Very God and Very Man. When we read in the Fourth Gospel that 'the Word became flesh', we must not understand, as earlier theologians did, a metamorphosis, a mythological happening, the coming of a heavenly Visitor; we must understand, rather, the total manifestation of the Word in a personal life.[3] The meaning of the Cross is 'that he who is the Christ subjects himself to the ultimate negativities of existence, and that they are not able to separate him from his unity with God'; so the Resurrection is not to be understood in terms of physical, spiritualistic or psychological notions; rather, 'the Resurrection is the restitution of Jesus as the Christ, a restitution which is rooted in the personal unity between Jesus and God and in the impact of this unity on the minds of the apostles'.[4] Death 'was not able to push him into the past', he 'brings the New Being, who saves men from the old being, that is, from existential estrangement and its self-destructive qualities'.[5]

(g) *Teilhard de Chardin.* There is a long tradition in Christian theology that the Incarnation and the Cross are a divine after-thought, a remedy for a situation which otherwise would have destroyed the divine intention in man's

[1] *op. cit.* II., p. 170.   [2] *op. cit.* II., pp. 153 f.
[3] *op. cit.* II., p. 172.   [4] *op. cit.* II., p. 182.
[5] *op. cit.* II., pp. 181, 174.

creation. The coming of Christ was, therefore, an intrusion into the course of Nature, the introduction of an intrinsically divine being into the course of human history. This theory stresses the indubitable fact that we cannot explain the person of Jesus by heredity or environment or in any natural way. It is, no doubt, true that we cannot explain the emergence of a Napoleon or a Beethoven at particular points of history, but the coming of Jesus as he is known in the Church and as a turning point in human history is yet more deeply mysterious. Nature is always producing new forms, but the dominant ecclesiastical tradition would remove Jesus as the incarnate Son of God from the evolutionary process. His coming was, so to put it, God's second thought and not his first.

But there is another parallel tradition that the coming of the Christ, the incarnation of God in humanity, was the very purpose of creation. 'The segregation of religion from science' is, says Raven, 'wholly incompatible with any real belief in an Incarnation.'[1] Life abundant is the goal of evolution, and life abundant is the purpose of Jesus.[2] In his posthumous work, *The Phenomenon of Man*, Pierre Teilhard de Chardin purports to trace the story of evolution as a groping, a 'guided groping', rather along the lines of Jan Smuts' *Holism*, but according to Teilhard there is something that corresponds to mind, to life, to embryonic consciousness throughout the whole story from star-dust up to man. At every stage we have in some sense and in some degree an incarnation of God in the material. As St. Augustine says *non ergo essem, deus meus, non omnino essem, nisi esses in me. an potius non essem, nisi essem in te, ex quo omnia, per quem omnia, in quo omnia? etiam sic, domine, etiam sic.*[3] This principle applies throughout creation. De Chardin

[1] *Science and Religion*, p. 197.
[2] C. E. Raven, *Experience and Interpretation*, p. 68.
[3] 'I should not be, O my God, I should not be at all, unless thou wert in me. Or should I not rather say, I should not be unless I were in thee,

points out that when any new stage is at last reached in the story of evolution, when particles coagulate into masses, when life appears, when man appears, there is no going back. So, we may go on to say, when Jesus appears, the man who, so far as human life may, is the undistorting mirror of the glory of God, there is no going back; a new stage is reached, as mysterious, as unpredictable, as decisive as the appearance of life upon this planet or the emergence of Adam, the putative first man; here at last is the Second Adam, the new man, the new creation, God at last manifest, so far as the incomprehensible Being of God can be manifest, in a human life; in the person of the New Man the Kingdom of God, to use the Biblical phrase, has come, and as life first emerging spread across the seas and then to the land and so into the air, the new life manifest in Jesus spreads gradually across the Continents in the chequered history of his Church. If the person of Jesus be regarded in this light, the old traditional terms can, it may be thought, without difficulty or distortion be translated into this new idiom.

In these and suchlike terms recent thinkers have attempted to speak of Jesus. In distinction from traditional christologies none of them offers an explanation of his person; they all abjure both metaphysical and mythological accounts of him; all assert his real humanity, but all are statements which point to the same spiritual intuitions as are enshrined in the formulae of tradition. To say of any of these thinkers that 'he denies the divinity of Jesus Christ' could only be the judgement of prejudice or stupidity. All are speaking language intelligible today and are seeking to provide a framework which will contain the unchanging intuitions of the Christian faith, that God was in Christ reconciling the world unto himself. The tendency of pious

from whom, through whom and in whom are all things? Even so, Lord, even so.' *Conf.* I. 2. ii.

men to shrug these attempts aside on the ground that they
prefer the firm and accepted formulae of the traditional
theological platforms must be resisted as a snare of Satan.
For purposes of liturgy in the inner circles of the Church,
of private devotion and of meditation, and indeed wherever
they have been explained, the old symbols may be treasured,
but let it be always acknowledged that they are symbols, not
explanations or definitions; as Tillich puts it, they must be
de-literalized, not de-mythologized.[1] But let there be no
doubt that the old mythological formulations, put out as
historical fact and revealed truth, inevitably alienate not
merely the whole Moslem world but all thoughtful modern-
thinking men from paying serious attention to the Christian
message, and lead them to regard the Christian's attitude to
Jesus as based upon a theory 'which some theologic bishop,
peering in the fog of his own exhalations thought pleasing
to God, altho' no creature might possibly understand it'.[2]
The traditional christologies are not 'untrue', but only too
often they positively prevent the modern man from seeing
Jesus.

THE DIVINE INITIATIVE

It is time to attempt some gathering together of this discussion. It has been argued earlier that through the touch of
beauty, through the mysterious and imperative claims of
loyalty and felt obligation, through the apprehension of
goodness or heroic virtue we become, or may become, aware
of God. Christians have become aware of God, who have
seen, as they are persuaded, the glory of God in the face of
Jesus Christ. If we may be said to know God through
beauty or our sense of obligation, our knowledge is not a
different kind of knowing when we know him through Jesus
of Nazareth. We must abandon the old distinction between
'truths of reason' and 'truths of revelation'. It is not 'truths'

[1] *op. cit.* II., pp. 175 f.   [2] Robert Bridges, *op. cit.* IV. 936.

in the sense of propositions that are revealed; as it is God who reveals, so in all cases it is something of the glory of God that is revealed. We could perhaps name many persons, mothers, fathers, wives, husbands, children and friends, through whom we have been made aware of God. What is the difference, if there be a difference, between apprehending God through our parents and apprehending him through Jesus?

Who and what was Jesus? Men have been aware of God before him and apart from him, but their sight has been dim, partial, intermittent. Jesus, to borrow Plato's metaphor, was Man emergent from the cave, clear-eyed and certain and beholding reality at last. Aware of a Father's Providence in the sun and rain, of a Father's care in the feeding of the ravens and the painting of the lilies, doing nothing but what he saw the Father do, saying nothing but what he heard the Father say, filled with the Father's infinite compassion for the sheep that had no shepherd, obedient to the Father's leading even unto death, trusting the Father when every human prop was taken away, trusting that through his obedience and agony the power and the glory of God would be revealed, truly 'the author and finisher of faith',[1] so one with the Father that 'Jesus is Lord' is synonymous with 'God is Lord', he was Man at last as man was meant to be, man in all the fullness and glory of manhood as the child of God, so one with God that in him dwelt all the fullness of the Godhead σωματικῶς, under human limitations. Hitherto man had been aware of God, but 'thou art a God that hidest thyself';[2] 'clouds and darkness are round about him',[3] nor ever was the darkness so impenetrable, a darkness that covered the whole earth, as on that afternoon when Jesus died a felon's death in agony, abandoned by his friends and abandoned, as it seemed, by God himself. Yet a few years later a writer contemplating

[1] Hebrews xii. 2.   [2] Isaiah xlv. 15.   [3] Psalm xcvii. 2.

the story of Jesus could declare that 'God is Light, and in him is no darkness at all'.[1] Such was the Gospel or Good News of 'Jesus and the Resurrection' or, as we might say, of Jesus and his Vindication. The heart and mystery of the Christian revelation is Jesus himself, not any theory about his person.

Mystery it remains even when we have abandoned all the traditional mythological and metaphysical accounts of it. Scientists can report, but they cannot account for, the formation of the first crystal, of the first unicellular organism, of the first vertebrate, of the first man. They fall back on some mythology of Nature or Emergent Evolution or Life Force. This is no less scientific and no less mythological than to say that these events were caused by the finger of God. It is quite 'true' that Mother Nature does all kinds of things, but when we speak of Mother Nature or Nature spelled with a capital, we should realize that we are using the language of mythology. It is quite 'true' that God sent his Son into the world and is no more, and no less, mythological than is science. But, as we desire an intelligible and rational 'philosophy of science', so we desire an intelligible and rational philosophy or theology for the Christian faith. Is there a christology available for us?

We must say first that the Chalcedonian definition, the Athanasian Creed, the Two Natures doctrine are 'true' in the sense that they attempt to make intelligible in the terms of patristic thought that which we must seek to make intelligible today. We may in the same sense accept as 'true' but reject as unsatisfactory and really unintelligible today the *kenosis* theory, which originated with Thomasius in the nineteenth century, and was revived in *Lux Mundi* by Charles Gore. The doctrine rests upon Philippians ii. 5–11 and is the view that, as R. S. Franks puts it, 'the Divine Son of God in becoming incarnate put into abeyance for the most part the Divine attributes related to the world, i.e.,

[1] I John i. 5.

omnipotence, omniscience and omnipresence, while he retained the immanent and essential attributes of Divinity, i.e., absolute power or freedom, holiness, truth and love'.[1]

There remains the Biblical conception of the Logos, the incarnation or embodiment of the mind and heart of God towards man in the person of Jesus Christ. It is very signicant that Kant, Fichte, Schelling and Hegel moved towards some kind of Logos doctrine.[2] Dr. Raven describes the Logos Christology as 'simple, coherent and sufficient',[3] and Dr. Franks says that the identification of Jesus with the Logos 'must still be the inspiring principle of Christian theology'.[4] In our own day it is Tillich who hast best attempted to express the significance of Jesus in these terms. Man, he holds, is 'made in the image of God' and, very obviously, mankind as a whole is estranged from God. Man, he writes 'is the image of God because his *logos* is analogous to the divine *logos*, so that the divine *logos* can appear in man without destroying the humanity of man'.[5] Jesus was subjected to the conditions of our existence without being conquered by them;[6] in respect of him 'the universal principle of divine self-manifestation is, in its essential character, qualitatively present in an individual human being. He subjects himself to the conditions of existence and conquers existential estrangement within estranged existence. Participation in the universal Logos is dependent on participation in the Logos actualized in an historical personality.'[7] It is thus 'the eternal revelation of God to man which is manifest in the Christ',[8] and Jesus as the Logos incarnate is the final self-manifestation of God to the world. We can say that 'in the fullness of time' life appeared upon this planet, and that 'in the fullness of time' man appeared upon the

---

[1] *The Doctrine of the Trinity*, p. 175.
[2] *v.* Franks, *op. cit.*, pp. 158–161.
[3] *Experience and Interpretation*, p. 82.   [4] *the Atonement*, p. 19.
[5] *op. cit.* I., p. 288.   [6] *ib.* I., p. 113.   [7] *ib.* II., p. 129.
[8] *ib.* II., p. 110.

planet, and that 'in the fullness of time' *der rechte Mann*, Man fully in the image of God, Man who, so far as a human life can, reflected as in a mirror the glory and redeeming love of God. We can state the facts; there is no explanation (unless it be the grace of God) that we can offer.

Our sight is still blurred and dim, but because of Jesus we not merely see, or have begun to see, all history and all nature with new eyes, but we have apprehended the divine initiative in our redemption to reconciliation with God and to forgiveness for all our sins against him and against one another; for Jesus was what he taught, his message and his life were one. His message would have been incredible, a mere idyll, a pleasing and heart-breaking fancy, had he not lived it in flesh and blood. Who could have believed in an infinite and indefectible love of God for every creature, had Jesus not lived a life of infinite compassion? He taught a delivering, redeeming, emancipating, rescuing love of God, but how could that be credible or revealed or even meaningful unless and until God manifested himself in 'that strange Man upon his Cross'? It is the simple truth that for us, for all whose eyes have been opened, Jesus has made all things new.

> Nature with open volume stands
>   To spread her Maker's praise abroad;
> And every labour of his hands
>   Shews something worthy of a God;
>
> But in the grace that rescued man
>   His brightest form of glory shines;
> Here on the Cross 'tis fairest drawn
>   In precious blood and crimson lines.
>
> Here his whole Name appears complete,
>   Nor wit can shew nor wisdom prove
> Which of the letters best is writ,
>   The power, the wisdom or the love.

It is because we have seen this that 'we know that the Son of God is come'.

Yet I hardly know, as Browning says. I am quite clear that for the purposes of proclaiming the Christian faith today the old Chalcedonian formula, the traditional 'Two Natures' doctrine, the Kenotic Theory will not serve, and that the Jesus of history was a real human being. Yet perhaps the phrase 'Very God and very Man', though intellectually unintelligible, is the simplest way of stating that which Christians mean. It is nearly true to put it that the significance of Jesus for history is very Man, his significance for religion very God. The 'Christ-event' as I have called it, took place through a human being, but what took place is as epoch-making in the history of this planet as the coming of life or the arrival of man; it is a new creation; it is a self-manifestation of God as personal and redeeming Love through the life, the teaching, the death and the vindication of 'the man Christ Jesus'; it is very God whom we profoundly apprehend; very Man is hidden in the obscurities of history, yet is not hidden in that through him and in him very God is apprehended.

VII—THE SIMPLIFICATION OF THEOLOGY

SOME theologies set out from Bethlehem and some from Calvary. The former lay primary stress upon the divine initiative in the incarnation of the Word of God, the latter upon his atoning work. This word 'atonement' is today unfortunate; it properly means at-one-ment but is popularly taken as a synonym for expiation, and indeed it is, and has been, commonly believed by Christians that Jesus Christ by dying upon the Cross made possible the forgiveness of sins by God, or (in an earlier form of thought) so 'gave the devil his due', that man's debt was paid for him. Whether man's debt, then, was due to God or to the devil, it has been regarded as an obligation which man could not meet but which was cancelled by the sacrifice of Christ.

To most men today the notion that our sins are forgiven, or need to be forgiven, 'by the blood of Jesus' or by some alleged mysterious transaction between two of the Persons of the Trinity, wherein one of them agrees to die for man and the other to forgive man's sins on the basis of this satisfaction, seems an unintelligible flight of fancy.

We must say first that most of the traditional doctrines of the Atonement, if taken literally, are incredible today; most are mythological, some are bizarre, and some, as it seems to us, immoral. All of them, however, are concerned with 'the centrality of the Cross within the event of Christ and of its symbolic power, not only to recall the event to mind in a formal way, but also effectively to express and communicate its central meaning'.[1] Jesus is usually represented either as

[1] J. Knox, *The Death of Christ*, p. 142. A useful summary of the various

the Victor over the devil or as the sacrificial 'Lamb of God'.
These are imaginative pictures which dramatically set
forth man's deepest spiritual needs, for deliverance and for
forgiveness, but, as Professor Knox points out, they belong
to different worlds of thought, they are mutually incompatible, and, if taken literally, are unthinkable.[1]

The Cross has also been interpreted in terms of revelation. The crucifixion of Jesus is certainly a grim revelation
of human nature and society. It was the religious bigotry of
the Pharisees, the worldliness of the Sadducees, the political
expediency of the Herodians, the fickleness of the mob, the
moral cowardice of Pilate and the indifference of the popula-
tion as a whole that led to this appalling horror. It is perhaps
significant that those in our own time who are most cynical
and most convinced that man, as one of them put it, is but a
worm wriggling under the spade of fate, are not wont to
illustrate their theme from the death of Jesus, since this
event by a strange paradox has become the symbol of hope
and of salvation, the supreme instance of the transmuting of
evil into good; 'it took over all the works of the devil and
translated them into the forgiveness of God';[2] for in the
Cross of Christ men have ever since seen a revelation not of
man only but of God also. It has opened their eyes and
brought home to their hearts the love of God and the forgiveness of their sins.

Jesus spoke of the love of God, but this had been a
dream, a fancy, *la délicieuse théologie de l'amour*, unless in
his own life he had incarnated it, manifested it, placarded it,
to use the apostle's phrase,[3] before the eyes of all the world.
'God's way of ending the separation between himself and
sinful men,' wrote Professor Burnaby, 'was not to wait till
men should return to him, but to go where they were *and to*

theories of the Atonement will be found in J. K. Mozley's *The Doctrine
of the Atonement* in the Duckworth series.

[1] *op. cit.*, pp. 144, 149 f., 152–156.   [2] T. S. Gregory.
[3] Galatians iii. 1.

stay there.[1] It was *God's* love for the world that was manifested in the death of Jesus who *was* his love incarnate in a human being. 'The New Testament writers cannot easily find words' (nor, indeed, can we) 'in which to express their conviction that in Christ God has broken through the barrier of man's estrangement from his Maker and brought him into the relation of a son to a father,' says Professor Lampe; 'that God has done this, that in Christ God was reconciling the world to himself, is the revolutionary fact which has turned all human ideas about God and man upside down, and is the essence of the Christian gospel.'[2]

We pervert the idea of God if we allow ourselves to suppose that God did not and could not forgive sins apart from the death of the Christ. John Baillie speaks, therefore, of 'the Eternal Christ who was made *flesh* in Jesus of Nazareth, and the Eternal Atonement which was made *event* on Calvary'.[3] We are not forgiven in virtue of some supramundane transaction, but we could not believe ourselves forgiven apart from this historical event. 'The crucifixion of Jesus,' said Donald Baillie, 'set men thinking more than anything else that had ever happened in the life of the human race. And the most remarkable fact in the whole history of religious thought is this: that when the early Christians looked back and pondered on the dreadful thing that had happened, it made them think of the redeeming love of God. Not simply of the love of Jesus but of the love of God.'[4]

The view of the Atonement put forward in these pages is that which is traditionally known as Abelardian. It has been treated with incomparable clarity, learning and insight by Dr. R. S. Franks in his small book entitled *The Atonement*. The Abelardian view, in brief, asserts that we are saved by

[1] *Soundings*, p. 229.   [2] *Soundings*, pp. 175 f.
[3] *The Sense of the Presence of God*, p. 202.
[4] *v. God was in Christ*, pp. 180–184.

the Cross of Christ as it awakens in us a response to the love of God therein revealed. This view down to the present day has been generally repudiated on the ground that it is psychological and subjective, that it reduces the work of Christ to a mere illustration of the love of God and thus cuts the nerve of the Christian Gospel. The objection is not well founded. It is a fact that from time to time rare spirits have believed in the love of God altogether outside the Christian religion, and that God is, and always was, 'a pardoning God'; the divine forgiveness, says Dr. Ferré, is universal in character and is 'a state of reality in which we participate';[1] but the abyss of the divine love extending to all his children including the outcasts, the sinners and the rebellious was not glimpsed till it was revealed on Calvary. Nothing can be more objective than that stark Cross outside the city wall. The Good News in its profundity is inseparable from the life and death of Jesus Christ.

SIN AND SINS

The idea of Atonement and forgiveness seems irrelevant to many in these days because, as is said, the modern man tends to regard the alleged sense of sin as 'the peevishness of a strict and illiberal education'. Much, indeed, that has been written by Christians about sin is morbid. We are not all 'miserable sinners', if by that be meant that we all normally and deliberately perform actions which we know to be wrong. Much Christian devotional literature foments a grubbing about in the soul whose humours and disorders become a matter of undue preoccupation. Some self-examination is very necessary from time to time, but we are encouraged to believe that when we turn to God in penitence, our sins are forgiven, that this forgiveness is to be adoringly accepted, and that our hearts are then set free for

[1] *Searchlights on Contemporary Theology*, p. 192.

the care of other people. Children are often naughty and know that they are naughty; when they admit it and promise to try to do better in the future, they are forgiven, 'and there's an end on't'. Sins are like that, though often they have involved terrible consequences for others, which, so far as may be possible, must be put right. But we must distinguish between 'sins' and 'sin'. 'Sins' are deliberate acts of wrong-doing, 'sin' is a state of estrangement from God, the source of our life. The modern man as a rule is not unduly oppressed by his 'sins' and would never think of describing as 'sin' the bafflement or frustration of which he is so conscious. Estrangement is therefore a better term to-day than sin. Modern man is conscious enough of being at cross purposes with his neighbours, with the life he has to live and with God, if there be a God. It is disillusionment, frustration and fear that overcrowd our mental hospitals, lead to breakdown and gastric ulcers, to sedatives, tranquillizers, sleeping pills and worse addictions. There is no dispute about the plight of modern man. The Biblical and theological description of his state is 'sin'. It is improper and unnecessary for evangelists to seek to evoke an unnatural and emotional 'conviction of sin'; men do not need evangelists to tell them that they are frustrated. To be reconciled to God, to one's neighbour and to one's appointed lot, that indeed would be salvation.

How is the death of Jesus relevant to this? First, in respect of 'sins' it is Jesus who awakens even in the best of men a sense of guilt. They may not have committed many acts of deliberate wickedness, but, as they measure themselves by Jesus, they become aware of undeliberate cruelties and blindnesses, of words left unspoken, of friends failed, of the needy overlooked. This realization grows on a man till he cries out with Lancelot Andrewes, 'all my life bewrayeth me', and with the apostle, 'who shall deliver me from the body of this death?' But this poignant sense of sin does not normally appear at the beginning of the Christian life; it grows. Christian in *The Pilgrim's Progress* has travelled some distance upon his way before he comes to that 'place somewhat ascending' where he sees the Cross, and there the burden is loosed from off his back, and he cries out,

> Blest Cross, blest Sepulchre, blest rather be
> The Man that there was put to shame for me.

Second, with that estrangement, which is called 'sin' in distinction from 'sins' the Gospel deals directly, for it is, to parody a modern scientific term, the way of psychosynthesis, which is best illuminated by the simplest illustrations. When I was young, it was customary for a child who misbehaved at table to be 'put in the corner' or caused to stand by himself facing the wall till he promised to be good. As a physical punishment this penalty was nothing; the suffering it imposed was spiritual. The family life went on, but there was his empty chair; there was conversation and laughter, there was eating and drinking, above all there was the happy unity of a family, but in this temporarily he had no part, he was 'in disgrace'. The Biblical and theological phrase 'to be in a state of grace' can most readily be understood as the opposite of being 'in disgrace'. When a man is in a state of grace, he is no longer isolated, burdened with a sense of guilt and outside the family circle of God's people.

The simile of a home also best illustrates the theological term 'salvation'. At home we are understood, we can be ourselves, we are sure of the love with which we are surrounded. Most men away from home 'put on an act', as we say; they wear a mask, they hide what they really are and most deeply feel; they are self-conscious, concerned with what others will be thinking of them, and therefore they are not free either to be themselves or to see other people as they really are. This lack of freedom shews itself sometimes in blustering, sometimes in shyness. It is only at home or with their intimate friends that they can relax and be themselves because there they have no doubt of understanding and affection.

The psychologists speak of our afflictions as inferiority complexes or superiority complexes; these are often accompanied by a conscious or unconscious sense of guilt. It is often quite impossible for the modern man to realize that the Gospel is relevant to his troubles, and is indeed the cure of them, because the Gospel in his mind and in the usual language of the Church is identified with a supernatural transaction or historical blood-sacrifice by which his sins, of which he is unconscious, are alleged to have been expiated or annulled.

It is often 'the making of a man' that he be trusted by someone who has his respect and reverence. Zacchaeus, the rich tax-gatherer, was such a man. It is the making, or rather the re-making of a man, when he realizes that 'the everlasting arms' are round about him, that nothing, not life, not death, not things present nor things to come, nor anything that he may do nor anything that may befall him can separate him from the love of God. With that profound assurance he is free. He is free from constant self-reference, from appearances that have to be kept up, from concern about what other men may think of him; he has come home; his heart is free to consider others whom he now sees with new eyes and often with a great compassion; he would 'brother all the souls on earth'.

This assurance, this conversion, this deliverance has come to men through Jesus Christ in the apprehension that the love and compassion shewn by him towards all men, and shewn supremely and finally in his dreadful death, so easily avoided had he loved men less, is a manifestation in time of the eternal love of God for all his children. This is not a probable Gospel; apart from the Cross of Christ it would not be a credible Gospel, but in view of the Cross of Christ it may be regarded as a logical and necessary Gospel.

THE LOGIC OF THE GOSPEL

For there is a logic here behind all sentiment. If the supernatural is only apprehensible by us through the natural, and if God is personal Love, how could he reveal himself to us as such except through someone who should reveal love to the uttermost? And, conversely, how could God be personal Love if he did not so reveal himself in flesh and blood? Thus Karl Barth speaks of the sovereign freedom of God to give himself to man, his freedom to love man.[1] When Paul, the persecutor of the Church, the associate in the lynching of Stephen, says of the Christ, 'he loved *me* and gave himself for *me*', he is gazing into an abyss of grace.

I write of logic here, but not of proof. How can the eternal, incomprehensible God, the Ground of all being, the Author of the galaxies, take the initiative and reveal his nature in a human being? A complete theory of *how* the at-one-ment of God and man can be achieved must lie beyond our reach, for we know too little both of God and man. But no new principle is here introduced into our thought. If we become aware of God through the contemplation of the starry heavens or in the silence of the great mountains or amid the sights and sounds and movements of a summer's day, if, indeed, we become aware of God in any way, it must be by the divine initiative, God revealing something of his glory to us through these outward media, as a friend reveals himself to us through his words and deeds and looks. In Jesus and in the Cross we apprehend, not a new kind, but a new depth of revelation.

The discoveries of the scientists in modern times have

[1] *The Humanity of God*, pp. 48 f.

fortified and deepened our sense of the fathomless wisdom and power of the transcendent God. It would be an absurdity to suppose that there is a God of unlimited wisdom and power but of limited good will. Using abstract terms we must speak of God as absolute Wisdom, Power and Love. But love to the uttermost, regardless of all cost, must be seen to be believed by sinners, by the outcasts of society, by men who have wrecked their own lives or the lives of others. God is always Love, but it is God apprehended in and through the Crucified that brings home his love to men, effects the at-one-ment and constitutes the Gospel.

On the Cross, as W. R. Maltby put it, Jesus Christ with arms outstretched embraced to himself the soul of every man for better, for worse, for richer for poorer, and death never shall us part, so that *every man* can say with the apostle Paul, 'he loved me and gave himself for me'. It is at this point that we apprehend not the general principle that God is love, but the saving truth for each of us that 'he loves me'. The Gospel is not the abstract truth that God is Love; it is the assurance that, in the familiar words of our old version, God so loved the world that he gave his only-begotten Son that whosoever believeth in him shall not perish but have everlasting life.[1] Put into the commonplace language of my argument this means that as in the sublimities of Nature or the beauties of the garden we apprehend something of the glory of God, and as we sometimes become aware of the Transcendent in the oracles of prophets and of poets or in the wonder of scientific research and discovery, and as indeed our ordinary human loves of family and friends have upon them the light of the illimitable and point us to that Beyond which is unchanging, so in the life and pre-eminently in the death of Jesus we apprehend a love of God that is to the uttermost beyond all limit and includes

[1] John iii. 16.

the publicans and sinners, the outcasts and the moral lepers. For my part I do not find it very difficult to believe that God loves everybody else, for even I find something lovable in almost every one, but the incredible Gospel is that God loves me, that neither life nor death nor things present nor things future, neither what I am now nor what I shall be when I die can ever separate me from the love of God which is in Christ Jesus.

THE TRUE RELIGION

It is because the Gospel can be put in these most simple terms that theology can be so greatly simplified and made intelligible today.

Rashdall correctly describes as 'the earliest creed of the Catholic Church' a confession found in some manuscripts of Acts but almost certainly no part of the original text.[1] 'When they (Philip and the Ethiopian eunuch) were travelling along the road, they came to some water, and the eunuch says to him, "Look, there is water; what prevents me from being baptized?" *And he (Philip) said to him, "if you believe with all your heart, it is permissible", and he answering said, "I believe that Jesus Christ is the Son of God".*' These words italicized occur in slightly variant forms; they were inserted, very early, into the original text and must be assumed to represent the primitive baptismal confession of belief. The formula of course needs and pre-supposes explanation, but when a man understands that which the name Jesus represents and what is meant by 'the Christ' and 'the Son of God', and when his consent is from his heart, then he has apprehended the essence of the Christian faith. Upon this foundation enormous theological structures have been built; these have crumbled and decayed; we stumble among the ruins. We shall find many

[1] *Doctrine and Development*, p. 89.

useful and shapely pieces of masonry in our rambling; these will serve us well as we try to rebuild upon the old foundation, but the building needs quite new and much less complicated plans if it is to meet the needs of the modern world.

'I believe that Jesus Christ is the Son of God' is not the whole creed of a Christian, but it epitomizes that element in his faith which alone is distinctive of Christianity. A missionary to French equatorial Africa told me many years ago that feeling moved to visit a village hitherto wholly unreached he stood before the villagers and said, 'I have come to tell you about God.' 'What!' they exclaimed, 'our fathers told us long ago that one day some one would come to tell us about God.' Their notion of 'God' will doubtless have been naif and unsophisticated, but dimly they had a sense of *God*. There is no continent from which we cannot derive evidence among the peoples we call most 'primitive' of some belief in God as the All-father or as the great Ancestor, the Giver of the customs and traditions of the tribe, the Guardian of justice and of right.[1] The most primitive custom of the ordeal, though of itself it involve no conscious sense of a personal God, implies the belief that there is a Power that knows the truth and will not acquit the sinner.

The Christian believes with the Jew and the Moslem that God is one; he believes with Ramanuja and the *Saiva Siddhanta* that God is love.[2] The Chinese thought of *Tao* and *Tien* and *Shang-ti* awakes an echo and response within his mind. If it be objected that in all other religions these ideal notions are implicated in all manner of false and superstitious and unworthy concepts, the same charge, in less degree perhaps but with less excuse, will lie against all the

---

[1] *c.f.* Andrew Lang, *The Making of Religion*; W. Schmidt, *The Origin and Growth of Religion*; R. Allier, *Le non-civilisé et nous*; L. von Schroeder, *Arische Religion*; N. Söderblom, *Das Werden des Gottesglaubens*.

[2] *v.* the chapter entitled 'God' in R. C. Zaehner's *Hinduism*, Home University Library.

Christian churches. 'That very thing which is now called the Christian religion,' wrote St. Augustine, 'existed in antiquity nor was absent since the beginning of the human race until such time as Christ should come in the flesh, whence true religion, which existed already, began to be called Christian.'[1] Elsewhere he tells us how he learnt from the neo-Platonists that in the beginning was the Word, and the Word was with God, and the Word was God; without the Word was not anything made that was made; in the Word was life, and the life was the light of men. Only this the philosophers could not tell him, that the Word was made flesh and dwelt amongst us, and we beheld his glory.[2] There is nothing distinctive of Christianity except Jesus Christ himself. 'Jesus and the Resurrection'—that is the Good News.

It is noteworthy that in the New Testament the first illustrations of true religion are not baptized Christians but Noah who 'being warned of God of things not seen as yet . . . prepared an ark . . . by the which he . . . became heir of the righteousness which is by faith' and Abraham who 'when he was called to go out into a place which he should after receive for an inheritance obeyed; and he went out not knowing whither he went'.[3]

All Christian theology is covered by the phrase 'the Word of God'. Only by an anthropomorphic metaphor can we speak of a Word of God, but it is only in human terms that we can speak at all. We are surrounded by mystery on every side. There is the mystery of Nature and corresponding with it the mystery of Reason wherein Nature is reflected; there is the mystery of Beauty and of Goodness, the mystery of human personality, and there is the mystery of

---

[1] *Retract.* I. xiii. 3. *res ipsa, quae nunc Christiana religio nuncupatur, erat apud antiquos, nec defuit ab initio generis humani, quousque ipse Christus veniret in carne, unde vera religio, quae iam erat, coepit appellari Christiana.*
[2] *Conf.* VII. 9. [3] Hebrews xi. 7 f.

grace. Out of the great darkness that surrounds us we are sure that God has spoken. We are sure of this because we ourselves, however dimly and however intermittently, have heard, as it were, a Voice speaking of that which is beyond this world of change and imperfection. It is not to Christians alone that God has spoken, nor is it they alone who have truly heard his Voice. God has spoken in many modes and in many fragments to men of every generation and in all religions, but in Jesus Christ we have apprehended his Word incarnate in a human life; his name is Immanuel, God's presence and his very self made manifest for our salvation.

This Word, incarnate in Jesus Christ, is the foundation of the Church, is proclaimed and conveyed in preaching and in sacrament, is the substance of the creeds and of all Church doctrine. This word awakens in us the apprehension that God is *God*; it comes to us in the apprehension that through Beauty, through Goodness, through the felt imperatives of Duty, of Loyalty and Love we are in touch with That which is beyond the world of transience and imperfection; it comes to us through the historic person of Jesus as the conviction of a divine Love extending to all creation and including the thankless and unworthy and polluted. The Word is God as he may be known by men, 'the effulgence of God's splendour and the stamp of God's very being'.[1]

It has sometimes been held that Christian doctrine revolves round the two poles of Creation and Redemption, the former being within the reach of the natural reason and the latter known only by revelation. A different view is upheld in these pages on two grounds, first, that though the sceptic or atheist may perhaps be led upon rational grounds to the view that there must be a Knower or Intelligence transcendent over or immanent within the order of Nature,

[1] Hebrews i. 3. *The New English Bible.*

only the illuminated or ecstatic Reason apprehends the universe as proceeding from God, as it is only the illuminated or ecstatic Reason which apprehends the grace of God in man's redemption; second, what we call Creation and Redemption are to be seen, not as different modes of the divine activity, but as moments in one single divine action, redemption being the end and purpose of creation. But we must also go on to admit that, while we use these terms 'Creation' and 'Redemption', we can mean by Creation no more than that all things visible and invisible have their origin and being in the will of God, and by Redemption we mean the spiritual home-coming of man who was made for God; what, if anything, Redemption may mean for the non-human aspects of the universe we cannot tell. There are two unique sacraments, Creation and Jesus, says Dr. Raven.[1]

There is no Christian doctrine which, if the reference to Jesus Christ be eliminated, is distinctive of Christianity. The doctrine of the Trinity, as has been indicated above, is a doctrine that God is to be personally conceived; doctrines of Saviour-gods and expiations are common in the history of religion, nor is Christianity the sole religion of grace, for Yodoism, a form of Buddhism, is most notably another.[2] This alone is distinctive of Christianity that 'the Word was made flesh and dwelt among us' in the Person of Jesus Christ. This we apprehend by the same gift of illuminated Reason, which may be called faith, as that whereby God is apprehended through Beauty and through the call of moral obligation as religious men in all ages have, dimly or clearly, apprehended him.

There can be no systematic theology in the sense of a tidy, comprehensive explanation covering the natural and the super-natural worlds of which we are aware. There can

---

[1] *Experience and Interpretation*, p. 105.
[2] J. Baillie, *op. cit.*, p. 189.

be, however, the beginning of a sketch of a Christian philosophy based upon the fundamental Christian apprehension that God is Love. This has been attempted in recent years by R. S. Franks[1] and Nels Ferré.[2] But while we can state what we believe, we cannot give a satisfactory and compelling answer to all the objections that may be raised against our view, for evil is a surd in Nature, not to be fully explained, though that of which we are sure throws light upon it. To this issue we must come in another chapter.

'AS LITTLE CHILDREN'

I have represented the basis of faith as the Word of God apprehended by the illuminated reason. It may be objected that this is far too intellectualistic a basis for a religion said to be suitable for all mankind, and that it represents that type of Protestantism which exalts the sermon as the means whereby the mind is to be illuminated, the affections kindled, and the Gospel brought home to the minds and consciences of men. The average ill-educated or uneducated man, it may be said, will never attain to religion through reason; he needs the authority of Scripture or the authority of the Church with its formulated doctrines and its sacraments; moreover, such an intellectual approach is inconsistent with evangelical Protestantism itself which demands faith alone, not faith resting upon 'the harlot reason' (as Luther so unkindly called it), which boasts its adequacy for the man,

> Who salvation sought and found
> 'Twixt the saddle and the ground.

I should reply, first, that I am dealing with a theological issue, not a psychological; second, that by faith I am mean-

---

[1] *The Atonement*, Ch. V.
[2] *The Christian Understanding of God*, *passim*.

ing not a virtue of the intellect but an assent of the whole personality, heart, mind and will. In Roman Catholic theology a clear distinction is drawn between faith, defined as a virtue of the intellect, and love. I am using 'faith' in the New Testament sense of *pistis*, which means a self-committal in love to Christ as Truth; it involves, in the Roman Catholic sense, both faith and love. Here, as so often in our theological disputes, an identity of meaning may be hidden under a divergent use of terms.

Further, the basis of faith is not Scripture, yet it is not apart from Scripture; it is not the Church, though it is not apart from the Church; it is not private judgement, if by that be meant the idiosyncrasy of the individual. Alternatively we may say that the basis of faith is Scripture as Scripture testifies to the Word of God incarnate in the Christ, or it is the Church in so far as the Church with its doctrines and its sacraments is a part of the Christ-event, or it is private judgement if by that be understood a personal and individual apprehension of that to which the Scriptures and the Church bear witness.

We are told in Scripture that unless we be converted and become as little children, we shall in no wise enter the kingdom. This entry is peculiarly hard for intellectuals. The Gospel is very simple; it is apprehended by the illuminated Reason, not by reasoning. Faith is an immediate perception, not the conclusion of a syllogism. Coventry Patmore says somewhere that having gone to bed one night burdened with all manner of intellectual insolubles he was awakened next morning by a peasant singing as he went to work; the words he sang were these:

> My God, the spring of all my joys,
> The life of my delights,
> The glory of my brightest days,
> The comfort of my nights,

In darkest shades if thou appear,
My dawning is begun;
Thou art my soul's bright morning star,
And thou my rising sun.

The opening heavens around me shine
With beams of sacred bliss,
If Jesus shew his mercy mine,
And whispers—I am his.

My soul would leave this heavy clay
At that transporting word,
Run up with joy the shining way
To see and praise my Lord.

Fearless of hell and ghastly death
I'd break through every foe;
The wings of love and arms of faith
Would bear me conqueror through.

The task of theology is not to spin theories about the Being of the incomprehensible Godhead, nor to offer a metaphysical account of the relation of Jesus of Nazareth to his heavenly Father; it is, rather, so far as possible, to present a systematic view of nature and of life implicit in the light of the direct perception of this peasant chorister.

VIII—PROVIDENCE

TRADITIONAL textbooks of theology deal for the most part with the great doctrines of the faith, the Trinity, the Person of Christ, the Atonement, the Last Things. These are themes which in the past have agitated and divided the minds of thoughtful men and are, indeed, of perennial importance, but they are not the issues which chiefly baffle and torment us in this scientific age. There are many who would like to believe that Jesus of Nazareth is God's Word to man, that God is Love, but who feel compelled to say that life as we experience it and read of it in the newspapers is incompatible with the claims of such a faith; to scientist and historian God is a superfluous hypothesis explaining nothing that cannot be 'naturally' explained; neither nature nor history suggests that God is Love.

THE IDEA OF THE MIRACULOUS

The question of 'miracles' was the *Streitfrage* or main point of controversy in the nineteenth century. This was inevitable. When scientists came to maintain that the universe is a vast machine governed by unbreakable 'laws of Nature', and the religious held that every statement in the Bible was to be taken as inerrant and literal truth, theologians were compelled to maintain that God was pleased from time to time, and especially within the period of Biblical history, to intervene in the course of Nature by direct actions which were called miracles. This was a very unsatisfactory position:

Think we, like some weak prince, the Eternal Cause
Prone for his favourites to reverse his laws?[1]

The controversy in this form is at an end. Theologians no longer regard the Bible as an authority on scientific matters and recognize that its writers were not historians equipped with modern scientific methods of investigation. At the same time the mechanistic theory of the universe can no longer claim to be scientific; the 'laws of Nature', as we now understand, are generalizations, not mandatory pre-scriptions which cannot be disobeyed. Particular events may appear intrinsically improbable, but if the evidence of their occurrence be sufficient, they must be accepted.

I have seen conjurers perform feats which seemed to defy the law of contradiction, for a hat cannot be at the same time both empty and full of rabbits. Psychical research and even physical research produce evidence which wholly baffles us. We are apt to call these phenomena inexplicable, but such they are not; they merely remain still unexplained. We hope and expect that one day we shall understand them. There are no miracles in the sense of events that can have no rational explanation.

But what do we mean by explanation and understanding here? If the conjurer would tell us how he did his tricks, there would be no mystery any more; but the scientist's explanation does not remove the mystery. He will trace for us the story of Evolution up to the emergence of living organisms; he may even achieve such chemical knowledge and skill that he can produce conditions out of which in fact new life emerges; but why these circumstances should give rise to life is as much a mystery to him as it is to us. The story of Evolution is not intelligible except in terms of that which we must call Intelligence or Purpose; this element can be recognized; it cannot be explained.

What, if anything, then, do we understand by 'miracles'?

[1] Pope, *Essay on Man*, IV. 121 f.

Of every event that occurs there is, if we can find it, a
scientific explanation in terms of secondary causes. It might
seem, then, that nothing is a miracle. But we are still left
with the question how we who apprehend God as personal
Love are to conceive his relation to the natural order.

James Boswell quotes an observation of Dr. Johnson to
the effect that 'to reason philosophically on the nature of
prayer is very unprofitable'. So it may be religiously, but
theologically prayer is a crucial issue. The reason why we
pray is that we cannot help it; but can we rationally expect
any result beyond some personal *katharsis* or relief to be
achieved thereby? Can bullets be deflected by our prayers?
Was our deliverance from uttermost disaster over the
recent Cuban crisis due in any degree to the prayers that
must have besieged Heaven out of many lands?

An able surgeon once told me that to judge by his
experience patients for whom prayers are offered have a
better chance of recovery than other patients. Suppose this
to be a fact, as very possibly it is, then it is a scientific fact;
prayer to God will take its place with the law of gravitation
as a natural law, and we shall not speak of 'miracle'. The
religious man will say, God answers prayer; the scientist
(who may also be a religious man) will say that prayer is one
of the causes that operate in Nature.

But it is utterly beyond us to have a theology or theory of
Providence, because we cannot form any conception of the
relation in which creation stands to its Author and Sustainer. We say very properly that in God 'we live and move
and have our being'; all Nature has its being in him who is
the Ground of being, whom we call God. But of *how* we
have our being in God, and of *how* all Nature is related to
him who is its Ground we can form no conception.

Since all Nature including ourselves has its being in him
who is its Ground, its Author and its Sustainer, and since,
as we know now, the universe is not a vast mechanism, it is

absurd to suppose that anything can happen altogether apart from God. I come back, therefore, to the obvious fact that every event has many causes each of which, so far as it goes, is a true cause. A single illustration must suffice, and for this purpose my washing machine, which happens to have been troubling me of late, will serve as well as anything. I take my clothes out clean and white. What caused this happy consummation? It is caused by their rapid agitation in soap and water. But I might equally well say that since it is electric power that agitates the soap and water, the result is caused by electricity. But going a little further back I must ascribe the result to the skill and imagination of engineers who devised the machine I use. But indeed I myself caused the whole incident by buying the machine and having it installed. I bought it in virtue of an unexpected benefaction of a generous friend. It was therefore my friend who caused these nice clean clothes. Why did he so bless me? I can only suppose that God put it into his heart to do this thing. God is the cause of my felicity.

My illustration may seem banal[1] but it is theologically important. I ask for the cause of my clean clothes. The scientist will give one account which will be conclusive and within its limits comprehensive. The historian will give quite a different account; he will accurately and sufficiently record my behaviour and my friend's and will add his sociological reflections; and I meanwhile give thanks to God. It is this multiplicity of causes which enables scientists and historians to explain events without any reference to God, and justifies up to a point the practice of the writers of the Old Testament who tended to neglect secondary causes altogether and to ascribe every event directly to the hand of God.

[1] The offended reader will find the matter discussed more fully and in more dignified terms by St. Thomas in the *Summa contra Gentiles*, III. 69–77.

These considerations in no way answer the question *how* God answers prayer, or *how* we live and move in him and have our being, or *how* he is related to the general order of Nature which he sustains; but the idea of Providence is necessary, not absurd. Mind or Intelligence informs the story of Evolution from the first. The Ground of all being is immanent, not transcendent only. Immanence is as mysterious as is transcendence;[1] but just as here and here through some touch of physical, moral or intellectual beauty we are aware of the Transcendent, so too here and here in the flux of events we become aware of the hand of God and may speak, if we will, of miracle. But in this case we shall by miracle intend not some breach of the natural order but rather that in this event or that we not merely apprehend that which scientist and historian can tell us of it but also have a glimpse of that Beyond which lies deeper than the appearances of things. In this sense we never truly know any event till we see it as a miracle, for we see no event truly till we see the hand of God in it.

IMMANENCE

The sole duty of the cartographer is to produce an accurate map of that part of the world which he is studying; it is not part of his task as a cartographer to consider whether this tract of country be beautiful or salubrious or rich. Similarly it is the task of the scientist to provide us, so far as he can, with an accurate map or plan or description of the natural order. He would be overstepping his bounds as a scientist if into his description he should introduce the name of God, for God cannot be studied scientifically. Indeed, it is not the duty of the scientist or within his compass to tell us whether the world be good or bad; he

[1] There is a splendid phrase of Albertus Magnus, *bonum est resonantia Dei in mundo*.

must be content to describe it as it is. To the Christian man scientific discovery is a mode of revelation as an unveiling of the pattern of God's world. 'Science therefore has no object of study except the action of the Word or, as the Greeks said, of ordering Love. Science alone, and only in its purest vigour, can give a precise content to the notion of Providence, and in the domain of knowledge it can do nothing else.'[1] The Christian who should presume to prescribe to the scientist what he may and what he may not discover would act as improperly and indeed irreverently as the scientist who should attempt a scientific proof that there is, or there is not, a God. But how is the religious man to think of Nature as described by the men of science?

We are apt to think of such terms as 'revelation' and 'reconciliation' as being distinctive of human or even of religious experience, but I am sure that Oman is right in seeing in the reciprocal relation of these two terms 'the whole story of the evolution of all living creatures'. As life first emerged from the watery slime, these early adventurous beings must learn to live in accord with their environment; as they more and more adapt themselves to their environment, they come to know it better (in whatever sense 'knowing' may be applied to them); the better they know it, the better they can live in accord with it. To learn to live on the dry land or to fly in the air is to adapt oneself to a higher environment. When we call man a rational or spiritual being in distinction from the lower creatures, as we suppose them to be, we mean that he has to adapt himself to a new and higher environment by learning to live rightly in it. An essential element in man's new environment wherein he differs from the beasts, lies in his awareness of the transience and evanescence of all things in the world around him, and a sense of transience is correlative to, and implies, a notion of the intransient or eternal. The emer-

[1] Simone Weil, *Selected Essays*, p. 52.

gence of man is a leap forward in the story of evolution, but it is still part of the story of evolution. 'Religion,' writes Oman, 'differs only by reason of a higher environment. If reconciliation to the evanescent is revelation of the eternal, and revelation of the eternal a higher reconciliation to the evanescent, that is only as we know all environment, which is by living in accord with it.'[1]

I find illumination here in D. W. Simon's *Reconciliation by Incarnation* which, I see, was published in 1898. He suggests that an account of the universe in terms of energy and process or of pattern and purpose closely corresponds with the traditional doctrine of the Trinity. The Father is the Author of all things and persons—'in the beginning God created the heavens and the earth'. The Word is Plan or Purpose or Pattern; the Spirit is Energy or Power. All existence is in some sense an incarnation of the Word or Pattern or Purpose in the mind of God; all things were made by the Word through the energy of the Spirit, and apart from the Word was not anything made that was made. This applies not only to that aboriginal star-dust or whirl of electrons or system of vibrations or whatever be supposed by science to be the first step in the cosmic order; it applies to all things that have existed, exist now or shall exist. As 'the Father' corresponds to Transcendence, so 'the Word' or 'the Spirit' here corresponds to Immanence. A flower, a crystal, a constellation—each in its own way and its own degree may be described as a brightness of God's glory, an image of his Person. Of course, it is a very limited and imperfect reflection of his glory, a blurred and inadequate image of his Person. In more philosophical terms, God is the exemplary Cause of all that is. In religious terms we may say that the divine Word humbled himself or 'emptied' himself in every part of the cosmos. If a flower expresses in some degree the glory of God, it is a self-limitation of God

[1] *The Natural and the Supernatural*, p. 470.

that he should allow himself in some degree to be bodied forth in this creature of an hour. The incarnation of the divine Word in Jesus is unique in that, as we believe, 'in him dwelt all the fulness of the Godhead under human limitations' but is not unrelated to God's normal and continual relation to the universe.

The Spirit is the source of all movement, change, life, energy, as the Word is the source of all pattern and all purpose. All energy is God's energy. As the Spirit is said to have brooded over the chaos in the beginning, so the Spirit, the life-giver, broods over all the succeeding processes of time. To everything as to every person it may be said, 'thou hadst no power unless it had been given thee from above', or, as the Schoolmen would put it, God is the prime agent in every action. But as there is imposed upon the Word a self-limitation in the cosmos, so is there also upon the Spirit. 'As soon, however, as the divine energy, either at the beginning or at the later stages, enters on its cosmic work, it ceases to be under the direct control . . . of God; not, be it remarked, because of a necessity imposed on God from without, but in pursuance of his own plan and purpose. In other words the divine energy undergoes a kind of *kenosis* or "self-emptying"; this latter relation of God to the world may be termed his immanence; the former his transcendence.'[1]

A somewhat similar view is expressed in more philosophical terms by Dr. Austin Farrer. 'We must believe,' he says, 'that God has acted in all for the best; how could we possibly think otherwise? It was for the best, therefore, that he made a half-chaos of self-moving, brainless forces to be the bottom and soil of his creation, out of which higher forms should arise. But then a semi-chaos, if it is to be itself, must be a field of limitless accident; and accident is by definition an uncalculated effect. It may be foreseen, pro-

[1] Simon, *op. cit.*, p. 33.

vided against, discounted, or profited by; it cannot be intended or arranged. It would be meaningless to say that God himself planned the detail of a chaos, or of a semi-chaos either, in its chaotic aspect. His infinite contrivance draws some good out of every cross-accident, and, as we have argued, a unique good. But he has not calculated the accident with a view to the resultant good. If he had, it would not be an accident, it would only seem to be one.'[1]

It may be inevitable that we should think upon some such lines, but the mystery is impenetrable for us. In a striking image Simon suggests that the relation of God to the world is like that of a mother to the unborn infant in her womb,[2] but one mystery is not explained by an analogy, however happy, taken from another. Yet because everything in the universe is according to its kind and degree an expression of the eternal mind, the eternal beauty of God, a partial brightness of his glory, not only is man θεῖον γένος, of divine origin, but the whole cosmos is akin to the Word, the Logos. This might seem a modern reinterpretation of the 'seraphical' theology of St. Bonaventure![3]

THE RECAPITULATION OF NATURE IN MAN

Simon goes on to consider the assertion of the apostle that it is God's intention to sum up or recapitulate 'all things' in Christ. This is an idea which the majority of theologians with eyes fixed almost exclusively on the salvation of man have neglected or set aside. 'Each animal,' a nineteenth-century scientist wrote, 'has had a pedigree stretching back through all geologic time since the dawn of life on the globe, and bears the mark of its ancestry in its own development. The phases through which it passes from the egg to the adult represent more or less closely, in

---

[1] *Love Almighty and Ills Unlimited*, pp. 163 f.
[2] *op. cit.*, p. 34.   [3] *v. supra*, p. 46.

more or less modified manner, the successive ancestral stages through which the present condition has been acquired. Embryology reveals to us this ancestry because every animal in its own development repeats this history, climbs up its own genealogical tree.' This may require some restatement in the light of further enquiries but will, I take it, be substantially agreed. After citing this passage Simon writes, 'may it not be said to be highly probable that if we could trace back the genesis of any individual man to its very fountain-head, we should find that he began with a movement of two or more particles of matter to each other, either according to the law of gravitation or to some prior law; that thereupon they cohered and attracted others; that in due course molecules arose, and then the internal motion termed heat was set up, which is the preliminary step to chemical relations: that thereafter arose the combination which manifests itself in vital phenomena; and that at last, after passing through a kind of vegetal stage, discrete though correlate forms of living matter coalesced to constitute the germ which eventually, after an embryonic development recapitulating the evolution of the animal sphere, issued in man?'[1]

Simon appends in a note some interesting passages from John Scotus Erigena; for instance, 'God made every creature visible and invisible into man',[2] or, as I think we might render it, 'God put every creature into man'. Again, 'not undeservedly is man called the workshop (*officina*) of all creatures, since in himself the universal creation is contained. See, he understands as an angel, he reasons as a man, he feels as an animal, he lives as a seed, he subsists of body and soul with affinity to every creature (*nullius creaturae expers*)'.[3] Life's great diapason ends in man. But if in man, then only in the perfect man. The purpose of the universe was that the glory of God should be manifest in human

[1] *op. cit.*, p. 25.   [2] *De Div. Nat.* IV. 7.   [3] *ib.* III. 37.

form; the world was made that God might be manifest in the Christ, who is the purpose, the key, the clue, the meaning, the end in respect of all creation.

This may be good Biblical exegesis but is not wholly satisfying for our present purposes. In the first place, the conception is too anthropocentric. We are not in a position to say that God made the Milky Way and the undiscovered galaxies for no other purpose than that the Christ should in the fulness of time appear upon this little planet. In the second place, it suggests that all that went before the appearance of the Christ is intrinsically valueless and all that followed him a declension or unsatisfactory appendix; in particular, it throws little light on evil and on suffering. Could the appearance of the Christ as the consummation of the ages, even taken with the limited number of those whose lives through him have been recreated, so justify the agonies, the tears, the hunger, the destitution, the oppressions, the heart-break of uncounted generations as to be compatible with the view that God is personal Love?

WHAT IS 'SATAN'?

It has been argued above that through Beauty, whether it be of form and colour or of character and conduct, and pre-eminently through 'the grace of our Lord Jesus Christ' we have been made aware of the Transcendent, the Eternal who is God. Of this we have no doubt. The universe, we may now argue, cannot contradict itself; with that which we know, that which we do not know must be consistent; we will therefore hold on to that whereof we are certain in full confidence that one day we shall see the whole pattern of things and recognize that what once seemed incompatible with the love of God was really consistent with it or even an expression of it. This is a legitimate position. If we are to philosophize, we must start from the points of our greatest certainty, and of nothing are we so sure as of the beauty of Beauty, the goodness of Goodness and the grace of Grace.

But if we would commend our faith to the modern world and master the niggling doubts that arise in our own minds, we must, if we can, probe somewhat deeper. There is in the New Testament and, it would seem, in the teaching of Jesus himself a tension or a contradiction. This is God's world; his is the gift of sunshine and of rain; he it is who paints the lilies, he who feeds the ravens and counts the very hairs upon our heads; yet at the same time this present age is subject to 'Satan', and the old collect is entirely Biblical where it speaks of the Son of God who was 'manifested that he might destroy the works of the devil and make us sons of God and heirs of eternal life'. 'Satan' here stands for everything in Nature or history which plainly or apparently contradicts the view that the Author of the world we know is a personal God of Love. What are we to say of 'Satan'?

'It is better to have a mind not fettered by mere intellectual consistency than to deny plain facts in order to be consistent.'[1] Ugliness appears as much a plain fact as beauty, misery as happiness, evil as its opposite, but it is also a plain and very mysterious datum of our reason that ugliness, misery and evil *ought not* to be; they represent disorder in an order that is intrinsically good:

> ev'n the poor blasted promise of desiderat fruit
> hath true relation to the absent beauty thereof.[2]

There is no tidy or logically inescapable answer to this question. A humility that recognizes the limitations of our understanding is an element in intellectual integrity. It is idle to ask why the universe is not different from what it is;

[1] J. Oman, *The Natural and the Supernatural*, p. 334.
[2] *The Testament of Beauty*, IV. 580 f.

we must try to 'make sense', so far as we can, of the universe
as we actually find it. 'Satan' is not to be explained or explained away. We must be content if we can begin to see, or
obscurely glimpse, how, as in the Book of Job, Satan may
somehow be a servant of the living God.

THE PRIVATIVE VIEW OF EVIL

There is, indeed, a philosophical account of evil which
in some degree is satisfactory. 'No essence is intrinsically
evil,' says St. Thomas Aquinas; 'by evil we simply mean a
deprivation of that which one should naturally possess, for
that is the universal usage of this term "evil". Now a deprivation is not any kind of essence; it is a negation within a substance. Evil, therefore, is not any kind of essence in things.'[1]
In other words, everything that exists is good in so far as
its nature is realized and fulfilled; evil is a deprivation of a
good that is proper to any substance. The lack of two legs,
for instance, is an evil for a man, because a man ought to
have two legs. But nothing is *intrinsically* evil, for to be
without two legs is not an evil in a fish. Blindness exists—
but as a deprivation of sight. There is no evil that cannot be
described as the absence of a good that should be present.
Therefore *malum non causatur nisi a bono*, evil is caused by
good; we may say, then, that evil has a deficient, not an
efficient, cause.[2] Evil, in fact, would have no meaning except
as a blemish in an order that is intrinsically good. Evil is
actual, but it is privative, not positive. 'All that exists,' says
St. Augustine, 'is good. And so that evil, whose origin I was
seeking, is not a substance; because if it were a substance,
it would be good.'[3] Again, 'I asked what wickedness was,
and I found that it was no substance, but a perversity of will,

---

[1] *Summa contra Gent.* III. 7. The argument is pursued through the
first twenty chapters of this book. See also *Summa Theologica*, I. qq. 48
and 49.
[2] *Contra Gentiles*, Ch. X.   [3] *Conf.* VII. 12.

which turns aside from thee, O God, the supreme Substance, to desire the lowest, flinging away its inner treasure
and boasting itself an outcast'.[1]

We can, indeed, always *describe* evil as the perversion
of an order that is intrinsically good. We can imagine good
without evil, but we cannot imagine evil apart from some
good which it perverts. St. Thomas' argument is valid that,
if evil is, then God must be as the Ground of an order that
is intrinsically good. But this approach is not satisfactory to
us, because we no longer think in terms of 'substances' as
the ground of evil, and it is not helpful to say of the
gladiatorial games or of Belsen that they are a corruption of
something good in itself; moreover, all those who give
themselves to the cause of humanity in any form are aware
of a very positive or, as it seems, 'demonic' power of evil in
the world. The slums are an evil in the sense of a deprivation of sanitation, dry walls and fresh air, but this external
account overlooks the spiritual *malaise* for which slums
stand, and to say that this *malaise*, whether in landlord or
tenant, is an absence of a good which should be there falls
far short of a satisfactory account. We cannot so easily
vindicate the ways of God with man. We turn back, then,
to the pain and suffering of the ages.

PAIN AND SUFFERING

Animals can suffer physical pain and mental pain in the
form of fright, but the tiger that leaps upon the gazelle is
not being cruel; it is only men who can, and often do, show
cruelty to animals. It is idle to think that the exquisite grace
of the gazelle or the supple magnificence of the tiger could
have been evolved in a world without struggle and suffering
and death. We have no reason to suppose that the life of
animals is unhappy.[2] As for man, it is written of Jesus that

[1] *Conf.* VII. 16.
[2] *v.* Raven, *Experience and Interpretation*, pp. 115 f.

'he learned obedience by the things that he suffered';[1] we all learn that way, or if we do not learn through suffering but are merely exasperated by it, we miss life's meaning and its beauty. '*Souffrir passe; avoir souffert ne passe jamais*'.[2] Coulson Kernahan once wrote a story entitled *The Man of No Sorrows*; this man's gifts, privileges, merits, benefactions and successes were portrayed; there was no need to draw the moral that he was not comparable in grandeur to the Man of Sorrows:

> So that for ever since, in minds of men
> By some true instinct this life has survived
> In a religious immemorial light,
> Pre-eminent in one thing most of all;
> The Man of Sorrows;—and the Cross of Christ
> Is more to us than all his miracles.[3]

Pain and suffering, unnecessary pain and suffering, as it seems to us, remain the great enigma, the surd in the universal order. Into this mystery we can sometimes see a little way, for we can deal with our own suffering as we cannot with the sufferings of others. Traherne writes of his monitor: 'he thought within himself that this world was far better than Paradise had men eyes to see its glory and their advantages. For the very miseries and sins and offences that are in it are the materials of his joy and triumph and glory. So that he is to learn a diviner art that will now be happy, and that is like a royal chemist to reign among poisons, to turn scorpions into fishes, weeds into flowers, bruises into ornaments, poisons into cordials. And he that cannot learn this art of extracting good out of evil is to be accounted nothing. Heretofore to enjoy beauties and be grateful for benefits was all the art that was required to felicity, but now a man must, like a God, bring Light out of Darkness, and order out of

---

[1] Hebrews v. 8.   [2] L. Bloy.
[3] Mrs. Hamilton King, *The Disciples*.

confusion. Which we are taught to do by His wisdom that ruleth in the midst of storms and tempests'.[1]

Where as logicians or theologians we are baffled, the poets, as so often, can let down a flickering candle into the abyss. I quote therefore again from Ugo Bassi's sermon in the hospital:[2]

> But if, impatient, thou let slip thy cross,
> Thou wilt not find it in this world again,
> Nor in another; here, and here alone,
> Is given thee to *suffer* for God's sake.
> In other worlds we shall more perfectly
> Serve him and love him, praise him, work for him,
> Grow near and nearer him with all delight;
> But then we shall not any more be called
> To suffer, which is our appointment here.
> Canst thou not suffer then one hour—or two?
> If he should call thee from thy cross today,
> Saying, It is finished!—that hard cross of thine
> From which thou prayest for deliverance,
> Thinkest thou not some passion of regret
> Would overcome thee? Thou wouldst say, 'So soon?
> Let me go back and suffer yet awhile
> More patiently;—I have not yet praised God'.
> And he might answer to thee,—'Never more.
> All pain is done with'. Whensoe'er it comes,
> That summons that we look for, it will seem
> Soon, yea too soon. Let us take heed in time
> That God may now be glorified in us;
> And while we suffer, let us set our souls
> To suffer perfectly: since this alone,
> The suffering, which is this world's special grace,
> May here be perfected and left behind.

To the rebuke that the generations of mankind with a few individual exceptions have suffered not 'for God's sake' but bitterly and often hopelessly because they could not help it there may be no reply, but we shall not judge that the poet here writes foolishly. Our imaginations are not strong

---

[1] *Centuries of Meditation*, IV. 21.   [2] Mrs. Hamilton King, *ib*.

enough to grasp the sufferings of men, women and children through long ages past and even within our own lifetime— through war, through cruelty, through disease, through hunger and through destitution, and when we are asked how we reconcile this tale of woe with the idea of God as personal Love, we have no answer except perhaps that what we do not know must somehow be consonant with what we know.

THE CONSUMMATION

The age of the New Testament was conscious as are we of the paradox, the contradictions, the agelong conflicts which make the universal order so much of a disorder. They looked for the ἀποκατάστασις, the Restoration, the παλιγγενεσία or Rebirth of the natural order.[1] This is the sphere of hope and mythology, not of science or of logic. The science of thermodynamics can make prognostications about the future of this planet. Man will not be here for ever. Religion is concerned with meaning. I will venture here to quote from an exposition of the Epistle to the Ephesians entitled *Christ and His Seed* published in 1872 and written by John Pulsford who was a pastor and a seer. It is sound Biblical exegesis; in no literal sense can we take it to be true; it should be understood as we interpret a great painting or as we enter into a great musical composition; any truth that it conveys is in the form of intuition, not of accurate description or of explanation.

'The grace which God hath made to abound towards us through his Son,' writes Pulsford, 'is no deviation from his original plan. All along, before the days of Chaos, before the angels fell and through all the celestial and terrestrial ages, God carried in his bosom a certain purpose, called "the mystery of his will". He always meant that his creatures

[1] Acts iii. 21, Matthew xix. 28.

should undergo a long, patient and manifold experience before he disclosed his central plan. The incarnation of his Son and his mediatorial relationships are strictly the carrying out of the design, which, before the beginning of his works, he had "purposed in himself" . . . From time immemorial the universe, from its centre to its utmost circumference, has been a house of division. Spirits are opposed to spirits, wills to wills, thoughts to thoughts, elements to elements . . . Add to this the awful division between heaven and hell, and you must see that the Cross of God is both a greater and more ancient cross than any of us can comprehend . . . Nature throughout all her kingdoms, bears witness to a universal strife, and inspired Seers bear witness to "war in heaven" . . . Our Lord testified likewise that the powers, signified by Satan and the devil, are ceaselessly working in opposition to him . . . But this strange thing called the material universe, what is it? Is it not an organized shadow of all that it conceals, namely, the strife between fallen and unfallen powers? Is it not strictly hieroglyphical of the great battle between heaven and hell? It is neither heaven nor hell; neither wholly good nor wholly evil, neither in accord nor hopelessly at variance with God. It is very anomalous. It is an enigma to all who think. In a certain qualified sense, it is a mirror of God; and yet no one can deny that it is one vast organized battle-field of contending forces. In many respects it represents heaven; but in other and manifold respects it just as faithfully represents hell. We call it Nature, *natura*, that which is becoming or about to be . . . We call her *mother* too, for she is in sore travail; and will expire some day in bringing forth the new heavens and the new earth, wherein God's truth and righteousness shall be seen again. Dying she will not die. Through her final redemptive new birth, she will put off all her vanity and put on the glory of God; her strife will cease, and her peace be eternal . . . Nature is one great cry for Christ's reconciliation . . . In the meantime the Cross of Universal Nature lies on the Son of God.'

This is the Biblical picture expressed in apocalyptic terms. Has it any meaning in these days? Apart from human history we have no reason whatever to surmise that the story of what we now call Evolution is one protracted struggle between good and evil forces; of fallen angels, of war in heaven, of a universal Cross we have no knowledge. But in human history we detect a *causa Dei*, an unending battle between two spirits or ages, the spirit or age of the Christ and the spirit or age that was before him and anachronistically is the age in which most men are living still. As the New Testament puts it, the powers of the age to come are already invading this present age; it is as if upon an enemy-occupied country its lawful king had landed secretly and summoned his faithful followers to be a Resistance Movement till victory be won.

This is edifying and important, but it is not philosophical theology. It may uplift the spirit and kindle the imagination, but it does nothing to answer the plain man's objection that the world as we experience it, and the story of man as historians record it with all its cruelties, oppressions, diseases, famines, separations and disasters, is incompatible with the view that God is Love. Here we are at a stand because we are required 'to justify God's ways to man' while the story still remains untold. We cannot be in the field of demonstration and must agree with Dr. Nels Ferré that 'if this life is all, faith in the Christian God of sovereign love is illegitimate'.[1]

BEYOND THE VEIL

But is it legitimate to posit a life beyond the veil of death? It is as impossible to disprove as to demonstrate that which Christians call 'eternal life'. In the field of psychical

[1] *Searchlights on Contemporary Theology*, p. 167.

research it is claimed by many that survival of death is proved. The general triviality of alleged communications from 'the other side' is not consoling, and in any case a mere survival of the experience called death, even if it were indefinitely prolonged, would bear no relation to 'eternal life', as Christians understand it.

It is very widely supposed today that the connection between our mental and our bodily life is so intimate that with the death of the body all consciousness must cease; the 'soul' is an illusion. Soul is a convenient but vague term, but if men contend that character and personality are illusions, they are twisting the data of consciousness to fit their theories, which is a form of intellectual dishonesty. Consider a human face as seen by Rembrandt or any great artist; the wisdom, the sufferings, the hopes, the longings of a lifetime are depicted there; 'soul' is a convenient word in which to describe this spiritual entity. What possible reason can be given to show that this spiritual achievement or realization or entity cannot be conceived to exist without a body and face through which very imperfectly to express itself? For we, in fact, are more than ever we manage to express, however mobile our features or ingenious our pens or soaring our musical compositions.

> But all, the world's coarse thumb
> And finger failed to plumb,
> So passed in making up the main account;
> All instincts immature,
> All purposes unsure,
> That weighed not as his work, yet swelled the man's amount,
>
> Thoughts hardly to be packed
> Into a narrow act,
> Fancies that broke through language and escaped;
> All I could never be,
> All, men ignored in me,
> This I was worth to God, whose wheel the pitcher shaped.[1]

[1] R. Browning, *Rabbi ben Ezra.*

Eternal life cannot be proved, but it is not an intellectual puzzle. It is a phrase meaningless or luminous according to the world in which each individual lives, for not all men who live in the same epoch live in the same world. Except in respect of things physical the dope-peddler and the artist live in different worlds, though they dwell in the same village. Where phenomena, which are appearances, are taken for the only realities, the spiritual world is deemed unreal, but in so far as we are conscious of that Beyond which is both transcendent and immanent, eternal life is not a 'problem'.

All human life is lived under conditions of time and space. The dimensions and conditions of disembodied life we are wholly unable to imagine, but this does not involve that we are left in total ignorance. When I wrote of an awareness of the Transcendent through Beauty in its various forms, I was appealing to an experience which, if not universal, is so common amongst men of any spiritual sensibility that I could hope to win immediate assent. Awareness of eternal life is less common or less commonly recognized. We must not claim that it is a distinctively Christian awareness, but for Christians it is coloured throughout by the self-revelation of God in Christ. This is one of the points where argument falls away and confession takes its place.

I accept without hesitation and in wonder and thankfulness all that the men of science, chemists, botanists and physicists can tell me about the trees that surround my garden. They either describe phenomena as these are manifest to the senses or they fall back upon *als ob* speculations; by this I mean, they say to us that things behave, or their experiments produce results, *as if* there must be the entities we call particles, molecules, electrons and the like agitated in such and such a manner; we cannot see them, but we can only 'save the appearances' or best account for our observations on these assumptions or hypotheses. It is through such observations, experiments and hypotheses that the practical technique of arboriculture is advanced. But as for me among the trees I am aware of sights and sounds and scents and the feeling through my fingers as I touch the leaves or boles. My mind most mysteriously apprehends these sensations through the stimulus of my brain which itself is stimulated by electrical discharges from the organs of sense, and these themselves are awakened by light-waves, sound-waves and the like. Of what is the *Ding an sich*, the thing in itself, which ultimately starts this process I have no idea at all. Of my sensations I am aware, but what do I *know* about the trees except what it pleases God to say to me through them? Reality is not substance; it is meaning. A poet and an infidel botanist walk among the trees together. Their sensations are presumably identical, but they are living in different worlds: the one is aware only of things, and the other almost exclusively of beauty and of thankfulness. In gratitude and reverence, in moral and aesthetic judgement, as Cook Wilson pointed out in a famous chapter, Reason 'can only manifest itself emotionally'.[1]

So we may be aware of eternal life, though there be no possibility of proving it. As embodied spirits we have to live in the world and *use* things for the practical conduct of life, but in contemplation we are only aware of other people and of God. Eternal life, as we call it, is a great mystery but it is not a 'problem'. A Christian looking back over his life is often filled with an overwhelming sense of gratitude that God should have given him such a father and mother, such a wife and children; he is conscious of having been born into a world of grace. If any should tell him that Jesus the Christ perished nearly two thousand years ago and has long since been dead and done with, it would be as if he were told that the night is dark when he could see the sunshine; for the Christ did not merely influence the homes that he

[1] *Statement and Inference*, Vol. II, ch. XVI.

has known; he constituted them, for they all revolved round him. He has brought us to God; he has reconciled us to the Eternal. And if he lives, they live also who live in him.[1]

We are living in a physical environment of the *actuality* of which we have no doubt, but the only *reality* we know is God and other people, and we only know other people as God speaks to us through them. We are living in a world where death is an actuality, but it is *umbra mortis*, a shadow, not an ultimate reality and for many even now their inner life is lived in a world of spiritual awareness unrelated to space or time. This is an experience, a way of living and experiencing, that we can no more prove than we can prove that the sun is shining, and no more pass on than we can pass on the ecstasy of a summer morning. Yet if this experience can neither be proved nor passed on, it carries a contagion. For Christians it owes everything to Jesus Christ, and we can help to open men's eyes to him.

But what has all this to do with the sin, the suffering, the agonies and miseries of mankind which to so many seem incompatible with the love of God? Much every way, as the apostle would say. If death were the end-all, and if there be an ultimate value in every human being, there is a contradiction between the alleged love of God and the actual story of untold human generations. But we as little know what death is as we know what life is. The story of Evolution is a tale of adventure, of struggle, of achievement through much suffering and pain; we can sometimes see in human history that the gain could not have been apart from suffering. We see this most clearly in the archetypal instance of the Crucifixion. It was not the will of God that Jesus should be rejected by his people, betrayed by Judas, deserted by his followers, condemned by the Romans and horribly killed as a common malefactor. Yet in the Garden

---

[1] *Quod Deo non perit sibi non perit, said St. Augustine.*

of Gethsemane he prayed, 'not my will but thine be done'. Theologians have sought to elucidate this paradox or antinomy by contrasting the antecedent with the consequent will of God. Antecedently it was the will of God that Israel should respond with thankfulness and obedience to the Word of God that came through Jesus; but when they would not, God consequently willed that through the sufferings of the Christ the eyes of all men should be opened to his love. Vicarious suffering for the sins, ignorances and complacencies of others is a law of human life. This is because we are bound up in the bundle of life together, and because we have to learn the way of love. In some true sense all suffering is a participation in the sufferings of the Christ. We cannot judge of the pattern till it is completed, of the story till it has been told. We do not know how God is dealing with any soul that suffers except our own. It is much too early yet to say that all this human suffering is meaningless. We do well to believe that what we now cannot understand is compatible with that which from our own experience we know, the unsearchable love of God made manifest in Jesus Christ. Faith is the only reason, but we must not call it proof.

IX—THE INSTITUTIONS

'THERE are three things, as I suppose, wherein the sum of human salvation consists, namely, faith, charity and sacraments'. With these words Abelard opens his *Epitome of Christian Theology*. 'Sacraments' in this context may be taken to cover the rites and institutions of religion. This is a field of widespread and often embittered controversy among Christians. Only a few generalities will be here in place.

HONESTY IN RELIGION

We may well set out from the solemn warnings of John Oman: 'to regard our opinions and practices as sacred is the only quite impenetrable barricade against the assaults of chastening experience . . . The absolute value of the Supernatural can be used so to justify our belief and to defend our judgement as to make tradition or preconception the very pillar of the truth; to give crude, hard, legal action and even cruelty and wrong the witness of a good conscience, and to clothe the unrealities of sensuous emotion and vapid sentimentality with the armour of piety. Refusal to enquire may be identified with faith; refusal to move outside the beaten track with virtue; and refusal to give reality any hand in our feelings with devoutness'. Again, in respect of 'religious experience', he says, 'this manipulation of feeling to make reality say, not what it wants to say, but what we want to hear, is the ultimate insincerity'.[1] Both Protestantism and Roman Catholicism afford ample evidence of this corruption. 'There is one proposition which the experience of life

[1] *The Natural and the Supernatural*, pp. 75–78.

burns into my soul,' said Gladstone; 'it is this, that a man should beware of letting his religion spoil his morality.'[1]

REVELATION AND DOGMA

Augustine Birrell, whose judgement in this matter may be regarded as unbiased, once observed that 'Christianity without dogmas, precise and well-defined, is more like a nervous complaint than a positive religion', and none will be found ready to defend what George Eliot called 'the right of the individual to general haziness'. A religion or a church must be based upon some definite beliefs. But what is a dogma, and what is its authority?

P. T. Forsyth says somewhere that 'a spirituality without positive, and even dogmatic, content is not Christianity; nor are gropings when stated as dogmas; nor is faith in the broad, general truths of religion'; but he goes on to draw a useful distinction: 'there is the theology which is a part of the Word, and the theology which is a product of it. There is a theology which is sacramental and is the body of Christ, so to say, and there is a theology which is but scientific and descriptive and memorial. There is a theology which quickens, and one which elucidates. There is a theology which is valuable because it is evangelical, and one which is valuable because it is scholastic'. Forsyth would have said, I imagine, that St. Paul's expression, 'Christ our Passover is sacrificed for us' is a theology that is a part of the Word, and the systematic theology of Aquinas or of Calvin is scientific and elucidatory. But the distinction is in practice hard to draw. Even so simple a religious statement as that 'the Lord is King' is scarcely 'a part of the Word' to a republican, or 'the Lord is my Shepherd' to an Eskimo.

A dogma, says a Roman Catholic theologian, is 'any religious verity which God has revealed in supernatural

[1] J. Morley, *Life of Gladstone*, II. 185.

wise and which the Church proclaims to its members and requires them to believe'.[1] But we do well to distinguish dogma from revelation, for the latter I take to be an unveiling to the soul of some aspect of the glory of God; it is therefore in essence non-propositional; it is the imparting, not of *veritates* but of *ipsa Veritas*, not of truths but of him who is the Truth. Revelation, as Tillich puts it, 'is not information about divine things; it is the ecstatic manifestation of the Ground of Being in events, persons and things'.[2] The formulae in which man, rightly and inevitably, attempts to express the revelation are secondary and subject to the limitations of human language and contemporary thought. 'You cannot claim absolute finality for a dogma without claiming a commensurate finality for the sphere of thought within which it arose,' said A. N. Whitehead.[3]

Every religion must have its creed or dogmas, but what, we may ask, was the creed, what were the dogmas of the Church of the Old Testament? As Dr. Phythian Adams once pointed out, the creed of the old Church, had it been formulated, would have run something like this: We believe in God who called Abraham to be the father of the faithful, who delivered us from Egypt under the hand of Moses, who entered into covenant with us at Sinai, who gave us the land of Canaan for our possession, who chose Jerusalem and its temple as the place of his abiding, who declared his will unto us through the Law and through the prophets, who, when we sinned against him, sold us into bondage, who brought us back again and established us in our land, and whose glory shall one day be known in all the earth. The creed of the new Church was a consummation of the old creed: God has visited and has redeemed his people; in these last days he has sent his Son; he has delivered us from bondage to sin and all the powers of darkness; he has

[1] *Religion in Geschichte und Gegenwart* ed. II. Vol. 1. col. 1963.
[2] *op. cit.* II. 192.   [3] *Religion in the Making*, p. 130.

entered into a new and better covenant with us; he has raised up for himself a new temple in the hearts of men, and we look for the coming of his universal and everlasting kingdom. There is dogma or positive teaching here, but it is in terms of 'the mighty acts of God', not in terms of theory or of metaphysics.

It was entirely necessary that the Christian faith extending into the Graeco-Roman world should, so far as possible, formulate and define its message in terms which that world could understand. The construction of theology is an essential function of the Church. But the Gospel in its simplest terms is 'Jesus and the Resurrection';[1] all Christian theology is but a commentary on that. It is Jesus Christ who is 'the same yesterday, today and for ever'; theology, that is, dogmatic statements must change to meet the ever-changing intellectual climate of succeeding ages.

What, then, is the authority of dogma? We do right to accept the authority of our church as, when we were children, we accepted the authority of parents. It was said of certain young men who boasted of their agnosticism that they had as little right to the solemn name of Agnostic as they had to call themselves Fellows of the Royal Society. Humility becomes us before the wisdom of our fathers; we may not reject till we are sure that we have understood. In the last resort, however, 'true humility', as Oman says, 'is not submission to human authority but total disregard of it when reality speaks to us'.[2]

We must judge our traditional dogmas and our theories by life and not seek to impose them on reality, as is the besetting temptation of ecclesiastical societies. If science

[1] Acts xvii. 18.
[2] *op. cit.*, p. 101. Because I can here say but little on this fundamental issue of the relation of revelation to dogma, I may be allowed to refer to my previous writings, *Reason and Revelation, a question from Duns Scotus*, to chh. II and III in particular of *The Abyss of Truth* and to the paper on 'the Limits of Agnosticism' in *The Place of Understanding*.

prove that the world is round, we may not say that the Bible
or the Church declares it flat and therefore flat it is. Again,
we must learn to distinguish a truth which we have apprehended from the setting, the context, the particular formulation in which it has come home to us. For instance, we may
not say, the holy Spirit is only given to those who accept the
Gospel as 'we Protestants' understand it, or is only given
through the sacraments as 'the Catholic Church' adminis-
ters them, and by imposing this view upon reality blind our
eyes to the else manifest work of the holy Spirit in other
churches. If one man's spiritual life be nourished and sustained by 'the sacrament of the altar' and his neighbour's
primarily by private Bible study and the public preaching
of the Word, it is very difficult for either of the two to
believe that the other has received the same gift as himself,
that if the chalice be different the wine is still the same.
There can, indeed, be no proof here, and no man's inner
life is identical with another's; but there is much evidence
that differences of theological opinion and church ritual are
irrelevant to that which is apprehended through them. The
hymns of Isaac Watts, of Charles Wesley, of James Mont-
gomery, of John Henry Newman, of J. G. Whittier, not to
mention the *Carmen Ambrosianum* or *Te Deum*, represent
the most divers theological and ecclesiastical traditions but
are a common treasury available to every type of Christian,
and the open-hearted recognize one another across all
ecclesiastical divisions. There is a promise in Scripture that
Christ will be present where 'two or three' are gathered 'in
his name'; our ecclesiastical differences cannot render this
promise of none effect, and woe betide us if our ecclesiastical theories prevent us from recognizing Christ when he is
present.

CHURCH ORDER

Empirical Christianity is divided into four main types, with many subdivisions, the 'Catholic', the 'Orthodox', the 'Reformed' and the 'Pentecostal'. All are imperfect as are all things human, and it may be maintained that some or all are seriously defective in respect of faith or order or, it may be, both; all stand in need of repentance; each has much to learn from all the others, and together they represent 'the Christ-loving armies' or the Church catholic in the world. It seems to us a tragedy of history that this Church catholic should be so divided, but it is not our personal sin if the sectarian spirit be not found in us, and it behoves us here to remember again the ambiguities of history.

Dean Inge once referred in a sermon to the historian as one 'to whom is vouchsafed the privilege, denied to Almighty God, of altering the past'. Ecclesiastical historians might seem to be especially privileged in this regard. We cannot read the past except in the light of our own experience, but an intolerable basis for church divisions is a claim to a knowledge of the past by faith which is not available to scholarship. This is a non-religious use of the term faith. There is probably no denomination that has not at some time claimed, with genuine but very limited justification, that its own church order reproduces that of the primitive church or even is as such of divine authority. In a well-known passage the late Canon Streeter compared this denominational rivalry to Lewis Carroll's Caucus Race where everybody wins and everybody gets a prize. In respect alike of the organization of the primitive church and the administration of its sacraments it is well that we admit our ignorance, since a claim to know what we do not know is one of the chief hindrances to Christian unity.

Historical evidence does not enable us to answer the question whether or in what sense Jesus of Nazareth intended to found 'the Christian Church'. Few today would hold that in his lifetime on earth he anticipated the development which we know as Church History. Heroic assertions of what he must be supposed to have said, as for instance in the alleged forty days between his Resurrection and Ascension, are entirely arbitrary and without basis in historical evidence. It seems clear enough that like the Hebrew prophets of earlier generations he came to summon Israel to its God-given destiny to bring the knowledge of God to all the world. That such a mission would involve 'Church institutions' of some kind might seem obvious, but in view of (a) the very fluid use of terms in the New Testament, (b) the issue of the relation of the Jewish to the Gentile Christians only slowly solved and that through catastrophe, (c) the very gradual development of the monarchic episcopate which we find established in the second century, and (d) the early expectation of a sudden ending of the world and the consummation of history, any exact instructions or legislation for the organization of 'the Christian Church' would seem improbable. If such instructions were given, they have been lost to historical research. We may, however, with some assurance lay down the principle that that church order will be best and will be divinely intended whereby Christ in any age can most surely rule the Church by his Spirit, and the Church be best equipped to fulfil its function. It may be argued that the papacy or 'the historic episcopate' or the Presbyterian order or the Congregational freedom, or some combination of these, will best fulfil the conditions of 'Christ's kingly government of his house' and best equip the Church for its service to mankind. It were well that the issue of church order should be discussed in connection with that principle concerning which, it may be thought, all Christians will agree, and should not be confused by arbitrary management of very inconclusive evidence.

SACRAMENTS

A similar uncertainty surrounds the 'institution' of the Christian sacraments. The rite of Baptism goes back to the very beginnings before Christians were called Christians; originally it was a baptism 'into the name of Jesus' and is perhaps to be considered a rite of identification with Jesus in his baptism,[1] but we have no reason to suppose that the original apostles received any baptism except that of John. The New Testament offers no clear evidence of the baptism of children nor, on the other hand, of the later baptism of those brought up in Christian homes; it has seemed to me entirely possible that when the father as the head of the house was baptized, the children would be deemed to be sanctified and thus virtually baptized in the baptism of their father.[2] It looks as if the early Christian Church assumed or carried on the rite of baptism almost as a matter of course. We are indeed told in the Fourth Gospel that in his early Judean ministry Jesus himself baptized at the same time as John, though this is later corrected by a note that it was not Jesus but his disciples who baptized.[3] We cannot suppose this to have been a baptism 'into the name of Jesus' at this stage; it must be understood as a continuation and extension of the prophetic ministry and baptism of John, which was also the baptism of Jesus. The roots of later and discordant Christian doctrines of baptism can be found in the New Testament; these must be appraised according to their congruence with the Gospel, but there is no evidence nor even inherent probability that any of these doctrines derives directly from Dominical teaching or requirement.

A similar obscurity surrounds the 'institution' of the Eucharist. The symbolism of the broken bread and the shared cup was familiar in Jewish practice, and we are to

---

[1] *v.* G. H. W. Lampe, *The Seal of the Spirit.*
[2] *v.* I Corinthians vii. 14.   [3] John iii. 22. iv. 1 f.

suppose that the Last Supper was for ever memorable, not because of a new ritual then inaugurated but because of the words then spoken. It is puzzling but cannot be of accident or inadvertence that in the Fourth Gospel there is no hint of what we call 'the words of institution', nor is it readily intelligible how they should have been omitted if they were as decisive and all-important for the Christian Church as has often or generally been supposed. Of these 'words of institution' we have five differing accounts, the Pauline, the Markan, the Matthaean and the shorter and longer texts of Luke,[1] and only in the Pauline version and the longer Lukan version is there any suggestion of the institution of some new rite. Even here the words 'this do in remembrance of me . . . this do, as oft as ye drink it, in remembrance of me' might naturally be understood to mean, 'whenever you meet to break the bread and share the cup, as you will do of course, then you must remember me'.

We do not know precisely what words were used, but whatever they were they must have been intelligible to those who heard them. All the accounts agree that over the bread he said, 'this is my body'. That these words could not have been taken literally is obvious, for he was bodily present with the disciples, and the bread was not his body. According to all the accounts except the shorter Lukan he connected the wine with 'the new covenant in my blood' or 'my blood of the covenant'. If he had asked them in any literal sense to drink his blood, every Jewish nerve in their bodies would have screamed. How, then, could the disciples have understood his words? Their Jewish minds were familiar with the symbolic actions of the prophets, which were more than symbols, for they inaugurated, as it were, the event which they symbolized dramatically. When

[1] Matthew xxvi. 26–30, Mark xiv. 22–26, Luke xxii, 15–21, I Corinthians xi. 23–25. The shorter and almost certainly authentic version in Luke omits in v. 19 the words following 'this is my body' and the whole of verse 20.

Jeremiah in the valley of Hinnom broke the potter's vessel in the presence of the leaders of Jerusalem saying, 'thus saith the Lord of hosts, Even so will I break this people and this city', he was understood by the elders and the priests not to be offering a rather childish illustration of what breakage is, but rather to be setting in motion that train of events which would end in the utter destruction of the city and its people.[1] When Jesus gave the bread to his disciples saying, 'this is my body', they would presumably have understood that in some new way he was actually and effectively giving himself to them; when he spoke of the new covenant in his blood, they will have understood, or begun dimly to understand, that in his Passion he was actually and effectively inaugurating the promised new covenant between God and man and was at the moment taking them up into it. This is indeed but surmise; we can only guess how each of the disciples understood his words, but it may be taken as certain that he spoke in a way to be intelligible to that circle at the moment.

The early forms or gradual development of the rite the Church came to call the Eucharist or Thanksgiving are obscure to us till we come to the account given by Justin Martyr in the second century.[2] We must not claim to know on dogmatic grounds and *a priori* what 'must have happened'; the 'eucharistic experience' of Christians, whatever it be, does not qualify them as historians. On the other hand, historical uncertainties cannot invalidate their 'eucharistic experience', though it may make questionable their eucharistic theories.

If the actions and words of Jesus at the Last Supper are to be taken as prophetic and *effective* signs, we are not shut up to the dilemma, either magic or bare memorial. The operation of sacraments has, especially in the 'Catholic' tradition, been regarded as miraculous. 'Modern science,'

[1] Jeremiah xix.   [2] *Apol.* I. 65 f.

wrote Inge, 'has inflicted a grievous wound upon this system by its denial of the miraculous . . . The sacerdotal and sacramental system of the Catholic Church is based on supernatural mechanism—on divine interventions in the physical world conditioned by human agency.' He adds in his mordant style that 'if these interventions do not take place, almost all that makes Catholicism attractive to the laity and lucrative to the hierarchy has vanished'.[1] But if Protestants believe, as they mostly do, that sacraments are not merely declaratory but also are vehicles of grace, they might seem to fall under a like condemnation.

The Christian conception of sacraments like all other traditional doctrines falls to be reconsidered in this new 'scientific' age. The crude idea of miracles as 'divine interventions in the physical world' is no longer open to us, but if for 'divine *interventions in* the physical' we substitute 'divine *operations through* the physical', the objection vanishes, and church sacraments would take their place in what we may call the normal order of God's appointment whereby the super-natural is made known and conveyed to us through the natural.

Their 'sacramental experience' is for many Christians so precious, so secret, so intimate, so mysterious that to criticize it, in the sense of asking questions about it and commenting upon it, seems near to sacrilege, but this reluctance must be overcome if Christians are to understand one another, and if intellectual and spiritual integrity is to be maintained. Christians are apt to say that at the Communion Service Christ is present in a special way and in an unique way becomes the food of the soul of him who faithfully receives. By this we must understand that Christians, or these Christians, are more conscious or are more deeply conscious of the presence of Christ at this Service, more aware of the Christ as their soul's food than at other times.

[1] *op. cit.*, p. 163.

Such a statement is not open to contradiction. But no Christian is in a position to infer from his own experience of the Christ at the Communion Service that another Christian at a quite different type of Communion Service or on some quite other occasion has not the same experience as his own, for that he cannot know. Indeed, such evidence as we have would seem to indicate the contrary. In so far as George Fox, for instance, and Richard Baxter and John Bunyan and Lancelot Andrewes and Jeremy Taylor and Thomas à Kempis and Bernard of Clairvaux and Augustine of Hippo, not to mention the author of the Fourth Gospel and the apostle Paul are able to reveal in words their innermost experience, we should judge them, in spite of all their differences, to be ultimately of a common mind and a common experience of the Christ. We should conclude from this not that matters of 'church order' and 'sound doctrine' and the Christian sacraments do not matter, but that the Spirit bloweth where it listeth, that any event may be the occasion of revelation, and that 'Goddes love is unescapable as nature's environment'; so Bridges put it.[1]

Any event may be an occasion of revelation or, to use Christian language, an occasion where the soul of man feeds upon the Christ by faith. All such occasions are 'miraculous', if we like to use the term; Christian sacraments are not more 'miraculous', but they differ in that they are events with no significance except that which they are designed to illustrate and to convey.

It is through the natural that the super-natural is brought home to us; therefore the Church needs sacraments. It should be remembered that preaching is as much a physical or material instrument as bread or wine; the same Word of God which is the Christ is brought home to men through preaching as through sacrament. There are, or there seem to be, some people to whom sacraments other than the

[1] *op. cit.* IV. 1420.

spoken or the printed word are confusing, distracting and unhelpful, but these are few and may be deemed unfortunate or even maimed. There is no limit to the number of churchly acts which are, or may be, sacramental conveying to the hearts of men 'the grace of our Lord Jesus Christ', but Baptism and the holy Supper stand by themselves, for the unbroken tradition of Christian baptism goes back to the historic baptism of Jesus himself in Jordan, and in the continuous tradition of 'the breaking of the bread' we are as those looking through the wrong end of a telescope who can see right back into the Upper Room itself on that dark betrayal night and are made themselves participants. The words 'this do in memory of me' suggest to us an effort to recall a figure ever receding further into the past, but this is to misunderstand the Hebrew idiom; to 'remember' in the Hebrew means not to travel far back from the present into the past but rather to bring the past right up into the present. So when the widow of Zarephath said to the prophet Elijah, 'What have I to do with thee, O thou man of God? art thou come unto me to call my sin to my remembrance, and to slay my son?',[1] she meant, not that the prophet reminded her of something that happened a long time ago, but that he so brought the past effectually into the present that, as she thought, it was causing her son's death. To 'remember' Jesus in the Biblical sense is, as it were, to abolish the past because it has become an actual and effectual constituent of the present.

That the super-natural is conveyed to us through the natural or sensible is a matter not of superstition but of experience. Eucharistic doctrines divide the churches; eucharistic experience, as there is good reason to suppose, unites them. I have no wish to modify what I wrote on this theme many years ago:[2] 'we may understand the Sacraments

[1] I Kings xvii. 18.
[2] Quoted by permission of the University Press from pp. 255 f. of *Christian Worship*.

of the Word if we conceive that at them the Church passes out of the space and time of ordinary mortal experience into a heavenly space and time. "The Lord's Table is the Lord's Table, and that Table is not made of wood or stones, nor is it many Tables. There is only one Upper Room. There is only one Lord Jesus Christ, Who hands to His disciples the bread, saying, 'This is My Body'."[1] According to the ancient use the minister at the Sacrament cries, "Up with your hearts!" and the people respond "We lift them up unto the Lord". From that moment it is conceived that the heavens are opened, and the Church on earth gathers with the Church in heaven—"therefore with angels and archangels and all the company of heaven we laud and magnify thy glorious Name". So, too, time is, as it were, rolled up, and that which in ordinary human experience we know as successive is seen in the eternal simultaneity of heaven. From the blood of Abel shed at the foundation of the world, through the sacrifice of Abraham on Mt. Moriah to the holy Nativity of Jesus Christ, Immanuel, His sacred Passion, his Resurrection in victory, His triumphs in the Church, His coming again in power and great glory—the whole drama of Redemption is, as it were, present together before our eyes as visibly occurrent, and the promise of our own inheritance is sealed by the Lord Himself upon our wondering hearts'.

THE CHURCH A PARTNERSHIP

Uncertainties about origins and early institutions do not qualify the importance of the Church. Under conditions of relative peace, prosperity and political stability in countries that have for centuries been part of 'Christendom' the position of the Church is equivocal; nearly everyone is Christian 'more or less', and nearly everyone approves in

[1] *Our Approach to God*, E. R. Micklem, p. 247.

general of the Church though its ministrations be usually avoided. To realize the significance of the Church one must see it under persecution.[1] But even here the ambiguous nature of the Church remains. As the company of those in whom the Spirit of Jesus rules or as an object of faith the Church is one, holy, catholic and apostolic; as an empirical institution it is divided, compromised, partisan, marred by worldliness and often far removed from the apostolic witness. Nowhere has this ambivalence or paradox been more clearly and passionately set forth than in the Roman Catholic Professor Hans Küng's book *The Council and Reunion*, especially in his chapter on 'the permanent necessity of renewal in the Church'. The Church is one, holy, catholic and apostolic in so far as the Christ lives in it; in its visible and empirical aspect it is an all too human institution.

What is the Church, and how can it be holy when its members, at least on earth, are still so manifestly worldly and imperfect? Enormous error and confusion has been introduced into this subject because Christians following the apostle Paul have spoken of the Church as the Body of Christ and have taken the Pauline metaphor for a metaphysical assertion. They have conceived the Church as a subsistent entity composed, no doubt, of individual Christians yet somehow possessing an independent life of its own. We often have occasion to make general statements about Britain or Germany or Russia, but these statements are not true of all British, German, Russian citizens, and there is no such being as Britain, Germany or Russia apart from the individuals who compose them. To use the technical language of the schools, a nation is not *ens subsistens* but *relatio*, not an entity in itself but a relation between individuals. Such also is the Church. No doubt any

[1] One small chapter of this story I have told in *National Socialism and the Roman Catholic Church*, Royal Institute for International Affairs.

church or denomination may have a legal quasi-personality; it may be *persona ficta*, as the lawyers say. But the Church of Christ is not a person nor an entity existing in its own right, *ens subsistens*, apart from those who compose it; it is in the last resort *relatio*, the name for a relation between persons and their Lord. It has the unity of a partnership, not of a substantial essence, a partnership, as Burke said of the nation, not only between the living but also between the living and the dead and those still to be born.[1] The Church on earth is the persons who compose it, and the assertion that the Church on earth or some section of it is one, holy, catholic and apostolic is a statement of what ought to be, of what is in ideal but is not in fact. The common assertion of Christians that the Church is 'an extension of the Incarnation' can be most misleading if it be taken to mean more than that the Church *is called* to represent Christ to the world and does in fact through its members to some extent so represent him; but if the empirical Church or the churches may be said to reveal Christ to the world, it is also sadly true that they often hide Christ from the world.

The Church hides Christ from the world in at least three ways: first, it so sets its highly speculative doctrine of the Godhead in the forefront of its teaching as to prevent its essential meaning from being considered by the Moslem world; it is often tied to an antiquated supernaturalism unacceptable to those with a knowledge of modern science; it declares its Western speculations to be the true religion and all other religions to be false. Second, it makes a false distinction between the sphere of the sacred and the sphere of the secular, being still largely Manichee in its thought. Christianity is, or ought to be, the most materialistic of all religions, taking material things, represented sacramentally

---

[1] This essential distinction, so important for law, politics and theology, between *ens subsistens* and *relatio* I have discussed at some length in Ch. XI on Corporate Personality in *Law and the Laws*, pp. 97 ff.

by bread and wine, the fruit of God's bounty and man's labour, as the vehicles of heavenly grace. It makes a false distinction between 'religious' and 'irreligious' people, forgetting that its Lord 'ate and drank with publicans and sinners'. 'This is the paradox of holy worldliness in the form of a servant,' writes Dr. Daniel Jenkins, 'that separation unto God is achieved only by identification with one's neighbour under God.'[1] Third, the Church has offered men a way of escape from the world and from 'the slings and arrows of outrageous fortune' instead of finding in faith the means to face and overcome the trials, the sufferings and the contradictions of human life. As the same writer says, elaborately organized forms of religion 'can quickly become a conspiracy against God unless the Church recognizes the insidiousness of her temptation to lead her members into a religious retreat from faith'.[2] As an unqualified indictment of the Church these strictures are quite indefensible, but it is well to see ourselves as others see and judge us. We are told in Scripture of those who could not come nigh unto Jesus because of the pressure of the crowds;[3] today there are very many who cannot come nigh unto him because of the distortions of the Gospel by the Church.

HUMANITY AS THE BODY OF CHRIST

To call the Church the body of Christ is in its place a useful and a happy metaphor—'whosoever receiveth you receiveth me';[4] but there is another saying, 'whoso shall receive one such little child in my name receiveth me';[5] and, again, 'inasmuch as ye have done it unto one of the least of these my brethren, ye have done it unto me . . . inasmuch as ye did it not to one of the least of these, ye did it not to

---

[1] *Beyond Religion*, p. 80.   [2] *ibid.*, p. 78.   [3] Mark ii. 4.
[4] Matthew x. 40.   [5] Matthew xviii. 5.

me'.[1] The body of Christ is all humanity with especial reference in Scripture to the hungry, the thirsty, the refugee, the shivering, the prisoner and the outcast from society. 'When a certain woman collected for interment the insulted remains of Nero, the pagan world surmised that she must be a Christian: only a Christian would have been likely to conceive so chivalrous a devotion towards mere wretchedness.'[2]

The Christ is the Saviour not of the Church only but of the world. In the language of early theology, he identified himself with all humanity , he 'took our nature upon him'; in him human nature was divinized or essentially and for ever associated with divinity; being lifted up he will draw *all men* unto him.[3] Can we translate this into modern and intelligible language?

Jesus is the incarnation or enmanment of the Word, the mind, the purpose, the heart of God towards man; so understood he is the incarnation of 'the eternal Christ'; he is also Man in the fulness of manhood wholly open to the divine. The coming of Jesus, therefore, marks a *saltus*, a new epoch, in the history of this planet comparable to the arrival of life or of self-conscious and world-conscious man. As all that which preceded the arrival of life and then of man is in a sense explained by that which arose from it, and as, once life has come or man has come, there is no going back, though, to be sure, this planet will not be habitable always, so all previous history leads up to the coming of the Christ and is explained in him. Once he has come there is no going back. The incarnate Christ identified himself with all humanity in its needs, its sufferings, its infinite inextinguishable hopes, because God always did and always does and always shall identify himself through love with all humanity, for God is love. The Cross of Christ wherein the

---

[1] Matthew xxv. 40, 45.
[2] From *Marius the Epicurean*, Walter Pater.   [3] John xii. 32.

enmity and estrangement and sin of man epitomized was transposed into a revelation of the divine forgiveness is the sign and seal of this. All the sufferings of humanity, therefore, are the sufferings of the Son of God; the Cross on Calvary is the appearance in time of the eternal Cross ('the Lamb slain from the foundation of the world'),[1] and all humanity is the body of the Christ.

CHURCH UNITY

We are rightly concerned in these days with Church unity. All the councils, committees, conferences, experiments to seek this unity have not been in vain. The Ecumenical Movement, as we call it, and the Council summoned by Pope John are clear signs of a movement of the holy Spirit in our time. But reunion cannot be a matter of mere formulae or ecclesiastical mechanics; three conditions are necessary in particular for its fulfilment: first, penitence; second, that the members of the various churches and Christian denominations shall be so obviously living in the power of the Spirit of Jesus that they cannot keep apart, and, third, that the churches shall think much less about themselves because their concern is upon the Church's task to bring the knowledge of 'Jesus and the Resurrection' to all the world. Church unity will be attained precisely as in fact the Church becomes an extension of the incarnation of the Word.

PRAYER

Theology is not unimportant, but it is holiness that matters most, and that depends on prayer. Holiness is the character of Jesus impressed upon another's soul; prayer is the soul's speech or colloquy with God. Here only such

[1] Revelations xiii. 8.

comments will be in place as may seem directly connected with the standpoint of the previous pages.

First, the man who has beheld the glory of God in the face of Jesus Christ, who either was born into the world of grace, or was brought into it in later years, must think always of the God and Father of our Lord Jesus Christ with a thankfulness and a happiness that exceeds any possible utterance. There is nothing he can do except be thankful—'what shall I render unto the Lord for all his benefits towards me? I will take the cup of salvation, and call upon the name of the Lord'. Inge rightly repudiates the notion that God wishes to be 'serenaded', and some forms of worship may seem to deserve that verb, but thankfulness and unmeasurable happiness in the thought of God are appropriate to the Gospel.

The Transcendent is apprehended in the Christ-event as a forgiving God. Self-examination is very necessary and indeed unavoidable when men consider Jesus the Christ, but the divine forgiveness is not something which, if we perform enough good works and are sufficiently diligent in the practices of religion, we may hope to receive as a guerdon in the end. God really has visited and has redeemed his people; when he forgives, we are forgiven; when as far as the east is from the west so far he has set our transgressions from us, then it is not for us to be always bringing them back again and reminding him and ourselves of them. True, we must work out our salvation with fear and trembling, and it behoves him 'who thinketh he standeth' to beware lest he fall, but it is the salvation we have received that has to be worked out. Every day we need renewed forgiveness for what we are, but *hallelujah*, not *miserere* is the keynote of Christian prayer and worship.

Third, while we must indeed pray for forgiveness for ourselves day by day and for help to see us through the days that remain for us, there might seem a lack of proportion if our own needs—which can be very simply stated, being in sum a prayer for the holy Spirit—should take up a large part of our prayer. Indeed, it may be thought that an atlas and the daily newspaper might serve us better than the more introspective manuals of devotion. 'I have set watchmen upon thy walls, O Jerusalem; they shall take no rest and give him no rest till he establish and until he make Jerusalem a praise in the earth.'[1]

Being the moody and unspiritual creatures that we are we need help, and we need discipline. We read of Jesus that he went into the synagogue on the Sabbath day 'as his custom was'; we need customs of that kind. We are, however, so differently constructed that we are in no position to lay down rules for one another. Perhaps it may be said on the one hand that the recitation of prayers or psalms to God, though an admirable spiritual discipline for us, does not of itself constitute 'praying in the holy Spirit', and on the other that to rush chattering into God's presence is a great irreverence.

Furthermore, it is hardly to be thought that the modes and forms of prayer natural when we are young will be natural and proper as the years advance (*pronus dum defluit amnis*). In youth the thought of death is far from us; we are insufficiently conscious of our limitations, and it is well with us if we want to put the world to rights. But as we grow old, our prayers for ourselves become much simpler: 'cast me not away from thy presence, and take not thy holy Spirit from me'—little more than that. We become increasingly conscious of the world's great need, but even if we are politicians, or perhaps most of all if we are politicians, we can only cry to God and leave it to him to answer our prayers according to the mysterious workings of his Providence, bringing good out of evil and turning the folly of man to serve his wisdom. Furthermore, increasingly as

[1] Isaiah lxii. 6.

those who are nearest to us pass beyond the veil of death,
and we become strangely aware of 'the communion of
saints', we come to think of death with other thoughts and
to conceive it as being

> only a step into the open air
> Out of a tent already luminous
> With light that shines through its transparent walls.

The mysteries grow deeper as the years pass over us,
especially the mysteries of life and death and grace. We
know so little, if, indeed, there is anything we know, but we
are very sure that from out the surrounding darkness the
nameless, unimaginable, transcendent God has spoken, and
to our deepest need has spoken 'in his Son'.

So much for the present must suffice. I began by saying
that we need a radical reconstruction of Christian theology
in these days. The pages that follow seem to me but a
starveling contribution to this theme. I have offered an
argument which makes no claim to be any kind of proof, but
which, as I hope, is congruous with reason, with our deepest
intuitions and, in substance but not verbally, with the traditional faith of Christendom.

My essay is little more than a commentary upon the
observation of Sir Thomas Browne in *Religio Medici* that
'we are only that amphibious piece between a corporal and
spiritual Essence'. We cannot infer the spiritual from the
corporal or material, but it is through the corporal that we
are, or we may be, aware of the spiritual or super-natural.
We cannot prove the existence of God because it is, in the
end, self-evident. Through Beauty, whether of pattern, of
conduct or of moral imperative, God has 'at sundry times
and in divers manners' made himself known to mankind
everywhere, but supremely and finally he has spoken to us
'in his Son'.

Following St. Augustine I have said that all our mental illumination, whether in science or theology, is a participation in the Word; this Word, which is, as it were, the uttered thought of God, covers all creation. All knowledge is of revelation or, from man's side, of discovery; in all revelation it is God who reveals, and it is God or some aspect of the glory of God that is revealed. How close are we here to the sublime philosophy of Benedict Spinoza: God is the true Substance, and all else is adjectival! But what I have written is not quite Spinoza, for, mystery beyond mystery as it is, we are not an aspect of God but persons, and 'spirit with Spirit can meet'.

In Jesus, as our hearts cause us to believe, the Word or Mind or Purpose of God is incarnate or enmanned so far as is possible under human limitations. Jesus was a real man. We must take seriously, where traditional theology has jeopardized, alike the unity of God and the true humanity of Jesus. The person of Jesus remains a mystery of which we can give no metaphysical account. For history he is veritable man; for religion he is Immanuel or God-with-us, for it is the glory of *God* we have seen in the face of Jesus Christ and the love of *God* we have apprehended in the Cross of Christ; in him we have recognized the divine initiative in our redemption.

The universe, as we apprehend it, is an order, rational and conative; *Spiritus intus alit*; it bears the signature of an immanent Intelligence; but the modes of the divine Immanence are beyond our fathoming. Pain and evil and the tension between that which is and that which ought to be remain insoluble mystery. But pain, evil and the constraint of duty we know best, and alone know intimately, in our own experience. If we have learnt that victory over 'the world' which is by faith, we may be content to await the explanation of the struggle till the age-long story has been told. Meanwhile we apprehend with the apostle Paul in the Cross of Christ the supreme instance of 'the wisdom and power' of God in the transmuting of human hate into the manifestation of divine compassion and the sublimation of human suffering into the means of man's salvation.

In my final lecture I turned from theology to church institutions, but here, too, the same principle obtains: the outward, the physical, the institutional is to be the instrument and vehicle of the spiritual or super-natural. This applies to questions of church order as to sacraments.

At last I came to speak of prayer as was inevitable and right. To discuss theological problems is delightful and a familiar device for hiding ourselves from 'him with whom we have to do'. I have come to understand the observation that it is for us not to speak *about* God but only *to* him. When we turn from theology to prayer and realize 'it is thou! it is thou!', we have moved from the dimension of the finite, the speculative, the transient into the dimension of the infinite, the real and the eternal. 'Behold, God is in heaven, and thou upon earth; therefore let thy words be few.'

These pages will appear within a few months of the fiftieth anniversary of my ordination as a Christian minister. I find my mind returning to lines I wrote not long ago:

> Full oft in youthful zest
>   I thought to teach
> My neighbours in their quest
>   Of truth, to preach
> And in effective wise
>   Evangelize.
>
> But was it for God's sake
>   That I could deem
> It no offence to take
>   Him for my theme?
> Was charity or pride
>   My goad and guide?

But ah, Lord, I repent
  My sin, thou knowest.
And yet was I not sent?
  O God, thou goest
Thine own mysterious way.
  I did obey.

No longer can I speak.
  Too bright, too vast
Thy wonder. I am weak.
  Thou hast surpassed
All words, all thoughts. I bow
  In silence now

And awful joy. But oh!
  Grant me, my Lord,
Once more before I go
  To speak thy Word,
Who live but to proclaim
  Thy saving Name.[1]

I could wish that this little book might be some answer to
that prayer. *Ipse concedat qui est in saecula benedictus.*

---

[1] *Verbi divini minister* in *The Tree of Life.*

INDEX OF NAMES